W9-BGZ-877

TALK IS (NOT!) CHEAP

TALK IS (NOT!) CHEAP

The Art of Conversation Leadership

Jim McCann

New Harvest
Houghton Mifflin Harcourt
BOSTON   NEW YORK
2014

This edition published by special arrangement with Amazon Publishing

For information about permission to reproduce selections from this book,
write to Permissions, Houghton Mifflin Harcourt Publishing Company,
215 Park Avenue South, New York, New York 10003.

www.hmhco.com

Library of Congress Cataloging-in-Publication Data
McCann, Jim, date.
Talk is (not!) cheap / Jim McCann.
pages cm
ISBN 978-0-544-11432-6
1. Management — Social aspects. 2. Leadership — Social aspects.
3. Customer relations. 4. Interpersonal communication. I. Title.
HD31.M38234 2013
658.4'5 — dc23
2013015266

Printed in the United States of America
DOC 10 9 8 7 6 5 4 3 2 1

Contents

Acknowledgments

Like many books, this one has a single author but a host of creators and contributors. I'd like to take this opportunity to acknowledge the many people who made it possible for me to run a company and write a book at the same time.

First and foremost, thank you to my family for their inspiration and patience: My beloved wife Marylou and our children James, Matthew, his wife Jen, Erin and her husband Joe. Thank you to my siblings — my sisters Julie McCann Mulligan and Peggy Hordt, my brother Kevin, who always brings a smile to my face, and Chris, my brother and partner in growing 1-800-Flowers.com. A special remembrance for my late parents Jim and Claire McCann and my late grandmother Margaret McCann for their support and guidance.

Thank you to my good friends at Allen & Co., including Walter O'Hara, a friend, mentor, and extended family member; Herbert and Herb Allen, the true masters of crafting relationships; and Tom Kuhn, friend, banker, and adviser extraordinaire. Also, a special thanks to a brilliant statesman, great friend and confidante, Senator Bill Bradley.

Many at 1-800-Flowers.com contributed to the creation of this book, but I'll call out a few who devoted considerable hours to its success. Thank you to Joseph Pititto, Vice President of Communications and Investor Relations; Yanique Woodall, Vice President of Public Relations; Jerry Gallagher, my friend and our General Counsel who always has my back; and Patty Altadonna, my irreplaceable, indefatigable executive assistant.

I would also like to thank those who came from outside 1-800-Flowers.com to join in the effort to bring this book into being. Thank you to my agent Joy Tutela of David Black Literary Agency for her vision and counsel. Thank you to the many talented and hardworking folks at Amazon, in particular David Moldawer for his editorial guidance, Larry Kirshbaum and Julia Cheiffetz for believing in the project, Carly Hoffmann for her stewardship, and the publicity team for guiding the book on its final mile to readers. Thanks also to Ellen Neuborne for her infectious enthusiasm and tremendous work ethic in helping to draft the manuscript.

Finally, I would like to thank the customers of 1-800-Flowers .com. Your support and passion inspire me every day.

Introduction

Some people make lists. Others take meetings. Still others meditate, searching for ideas and inspiration. Me? I like to talk. Conversations are my way of exploring, imagining, hashing things out, and bouncing my ideas off others while seeking theirs. Throughout my career as an entrepreneur, I have used meaningful conversation as a key management and leadership tool. It works. And I will show you how it can work for you.

Conversation is an opportunity created among two or more human beings to share and explore ideas. Leadership is the ability to recognize potential and propel situations forward. When you pair conversation and leadership, you engage others in a process of opportunity and momentum — a key element of starting any relationship, be it business or personal. That moment of connection brings aspirations to the surface and creates social intimacy. When this happens, a conversation can transcend the water cooler or the cocktail party and lead to some of the most significant accomplishments imaginable.

This is the moment at which conversation becomes conversation leadership. I coined the term to describe the process I've developed to engage with others and not just give orders or advice, but use the ebb and flow of conversation to create forward momentum. It has been the most powerful leadership tool I use. Through the art of conversation leadership, we develop the ability to unearth possibilities, feed off the enthusiasm of others, see ideas from different perspectives, and ultimately accomplish some pretty incredible and memorable things. Along the way, conversation can help us encourage and empower others to do the same. Isn't that what leadership is all about?

Within this book, I will teach you a skill set for an activity most of us take for granted. Conversation leadership is not a talent reserved for the lucky few with special gifts; it is a process that is accessible to anyone. Most of us are halfway there — we just need to recognize what it is that we're already doing and to refine our techniques.

Not every great leader is a great conversationalist. There are men and women who draw success from a unique talent or significant intellectual gift that has little or nothing to do with communication. These people have the drive and talent to accomplish the amazing without asking the people around them for much help. We are lucky to have these individuals among us, but they are a rare breed. The rest of us have to make do with good old-fashioned social skills. We need to bounce ideas off others. We need to search doggedly for someone who can help us realize our aspirations, and who sees good reasons to do so. During that search, we'll talk to dozens of people who seemingly aren't that person. The beauty of conversation leadership is that these "extraneous" conversations will nevertheless introduce us to wonderful opportunities that we may never previously have considered.

Inside and outside the boardroom, I have seen passionate, intelligent conversations drive great ideas forward. Conversation is the unsung supertool of human interaction. In this book, I will pull back the curtain on what I call conversation leadership: the use of conversation to foster success of all kinds — personal and professional, large and small. This process has worked for me, and so I have begun to share it with my staff, my colleagues, and the wider business world.

I have had thousands of conversations in my life, enriching and thought-provoking conversations with the famous (Wayne Huizenga, Jeff Bezos, Mark Zuckerberg, and Steve Case, to name a few) and the not so famous (my grandmother Margaret; the folks who do my dry cleaning; and Bob, the new employee in our service center). Yet as diverse as my discussions and the people I have enjoyed them with have been, they all have one thing in common: I've learned something from each and every one of them.

This book will take you inside the process of conversation leadership. Through my own experiences, I will explain how to use the power of conversation to create opportunities both in business and in life. To begin with, there are certain principles that I feel are very important to every leader. For instance: *Converse — even if you think you can't.* Conversation leadership requires patience and practice. I was shy, and I had to put great effort into developing my communication skills, but to say it was "worth it" does not even explain a fraction of the enrichment conversation leadership has brought into my life.

Another principle is: *Leave your judgments at the door.* Sure, it's easy to be impressed by the slick B-school grad with the fancy college tie and the four-thousand-dollar suit, but that pedigree doesn't guarantee that he will have the right solution to every problem. Back when I had my first flower shop in New York City, customers would come in, everyday people with everyday lives, and many of them would share homespun pearls of wisdom about the importance of relationships and how making mistakes is not only human but essential to learning and improving. These conversations provided insights that I continue to live by today, nearly forty years later.

Another key principle is very simple but sometimes hard to do: *Shut up and listen!* We all have a tendency to concentrate on what we're going to say next. Business leaders in particular are often expected to dominate the discussion. But falling under the siren spell of your own voice is a sure way to miss out on the true benefits of conversation. I have always learned the most by simply starting a discussion and then letting others take it from there.

One example of conversation leadership that I would like to share with you revolves around a philosophy that is close to my heart and my business. My brother Chris, who is president of 1-800-Flowers.com, and I have often discussed the concept of "conscious capitalism." This ideal joins capitalism and philanthropy in a way that creates a path to doing well in business while also doing good for our communities and for society as a whole.

When talking about conscious capitalism, Chris and I keep coming back to the theme we use to describe our company: We're in a good business. As a provider of beautiful flowers, gourmet baskets, and other thoughtful gifts, we're in the business of "delivering smiles," as we say. Of course, as a publicly owned company, we work to grow our profits each year and create value for our shareholders. Still, we also have an opportunity and an obligation to engage with all of our constituencies, from shareholders and vendors to employees and customers across the country, and to make a difference in the communities in which we live and work.

Toward this ideal of conscious capitalism, I recently began to seek out conversations with business associates, friends, employees, and others whose opinions and thoughts I value, looking for a way to focus all the various and wonderful initiatives that we do throughout the company and as individuals. Could we find a way to combine our efforts and put more wood behind the right arrow to take our philanthropic efforts to the next level and beyond?

During these conversations, more than one person pointed out that such an opportunity may already exist in a program we have been involved with for many years. Almost fifteen years ago, Chris and I helped build a greenhouse for our brother Kevin, who is developmentally disabled, and his fellow residents at a group living home on Long Island to grow flowers and plants to be sold to local florists. The Flower Barn provides meaningful work for dozens of developmentally disabled people, enriching their lives in the process.

Why not expand on this concept, these people suggested, and build Flower Barns in communities all over the country? As a result of the conversations I had with everyone from a former president of the United States to my dentist, Gerry, I was able to define and launch the perfect vehicle for our efforts toward conscious capitalism. Today, we are in the process of building an organization and working with community leaders across America to roll out the Flower Barn concept, which we are calling Smile Farms, nationwide.

Now I'd like you to ask yourself: What can conversation do for you? How can it help you become a better leader in your business, your industry, your family, and your life? What kind of effect can you have on the world and your place in it? Can you see yourself taking an existing skill or idea and refining it so you can use it to join with others and achieve great feats?

If so, let's talk some more — and see where the conversation leads us.

TALK IS (NOT!) CHEAP

1

—

Entrepreneurial Conversations

SOME PEOPLE ARE BORN entrepreneurs. They open their first lemonade stand at nine, and by age eleven have franchises in three neighborhoods and half the fifth grade on the payroll. These are entrepreneurs who make millions and then cash out to do it all over again. They can't help it. They love the chase.

Others enter the entrepreneurial space backed by an affluent upbringing. Well-heeled and well-educated, they hatch their business plans and then make the rounds of Dad's country club seeking funding. They were born into the golden circle of networking.

Then there's the rest of us. We are the entrepreneurs who stumbled into the space without the benefit of either the Ivy League or a supernatural sixth sense. We are the folks who'd always thought we'd work for someone else but it just didn't turn out that way. We are the accidental entrepreneurs.

And we have a secret.

In this chapter, I'll review the art of using conversation to start and build a business. It's such a simple idea that many overlook it — it's not nearly as sexy a concept as you'd find in curriculums at our nation's finest institutions of learning. But as I look back on the critical junctures in my own entrepreneurial career, I see that the turning points often took place in moments of dialogue — moments when I looked across the table at another human being and one of us said, "You know, I was thinking . . ."

It's conversation that starts the business. It's conversation that builds the business. It's conversation that turns your fledgling project into a going concern. That's what we'll review in this chapter. Because, unlike an inborn talent or family money, conversation skills can be acquired anytime.

A Guy Walks into a Bar . . .

I decided to build my conversation chops as a young man in New York City. I was naturally shy, so I thought a job as a bartender might be a good place for me to work on that particular soft spot. It was. Nobody ever wonders if the bartender might be shy. People just walk in, order a drink, and in many cases strike up a conversation. There was no time for me to ponder my reticence. I just talked back. It was a job requirement and I needed a job.

It was over the bar one night that I learned from the owner of the flower shop up the street that he was thinking of selling. It was not a spectacular retail location — a storefront on First Avenue at East Sixty-second Street. But it was a nice neighborhood location. As I conversed with my customer, an idea began to take shape in my mind. Soon after, I made the investment. That was my entry into the Manhattan retail market.

Conversation is the hidden key to entrepreneurial success. We all talk all the time. Even those of us who are shy manage to come up with a few words here and there for those we know and trust. But how often are we truly *in conversation*? By that I mean, how often are we talking and then listening and then moving the dialogue forward — giving the exchange some attention rather than just shooting the breeze?

For the accidental entrepreneur — the business-starter who does not come to the table with an innate talent or plenty of family money — the conversation may be the turning point. Many times I see young people at networking events or business conferences talking to one another — exchanging pleasantries, shooting the breeze, just filling up the empty space between them until the meeting or the presentation or whatever entertainment is on hand starts up again. I want to go over and shake them, and tell them to stop talking and start conversing. Start listening to each other. Start asking questions to get more information, more detail, more anything. Sure, this particular exchange might not lead you anywhere. But it might also be like that seemingly innocuous conversation I had with a regular customer about his plans to sell his store. It might be the conversation that launches your business.

Conversations that start a business don't come with flashing lights to get your attention and give you time to prepare — you have to be ready to have that conversation when it happens. You have to be open to the idea that it could happen anytime. You have to put yourself in a position so that conversations are possible — be out and about, be in places where people will engage with you. Obviously, it doesn't have to be a bar, but think of that natural conversation hub as your model. If you want to be a successful entrepreneur, consider the lesson of the bartender. Is your current situation one in which you are in contact and conversation with as many people as the average bartender is? If not, what can you do to fix that? How can you get out more, mix more, find yourself in more conversations more often?

Building a Business with Conversation

Most new businesses fail. If you've already started one, one of my most important tips is to continue the conversations around you. You need all the help you can get.

Some of it will come in the form of good old-fashioned advice. Although I started my retail flower business in 1976, it was many years before I gave up my "day job" in social services as a counselor in a boys' home in Queens. So many of the conversations I had at the home informed my business decisions. I often tell the story of the time, early on in my social worker days, when I was despairing to Brother Tom of my inability to connect with the kids. I wasn't getting through to them; I wasn't helping them the way I knew they needed to be helped. I was not cut out for the job, I told him.

He listened patiently. And then he said, "Jim, you need to go in with a plan. Not for life, but for the day."

We were talking about managing troubled boys. But Brother Tom's advice applies to any entrepreneur. The tendency when you start your own business is to shoot for the stars. We all want to make it big. But by focusing on that distant goal, we may lose hope. It seems so unattainable, so crazy, so impossible. It's enough to make anyone say, "I'll never make it. This was a stupid idea." It may not be stupid or unattainable — you may simply be getting ahead of yourself. As Brother Tom pointed out to me so simply, going in each day with the goal of "fixing" each boy right then and there was just too big. I needed to arrive each day not with a plan for my life, but with a plan for the day. Lay out the executable steps, go through them with precision and care, and move yourself in the direction of your goal without expecting to arrive in one great leap.

Other advice you gather will be more directly related to your business. When I was a young kid growing up in Queens, I met one of the most important business role models of my life. Of course, I didn't know it then or for years afterward. But watching him work was highly influential. So much so that his is a story I often tell today.

His name was Dave, and he delivered in the neighborhood for Sealtest Dairy — a division of a bigger company that would eventually go on to become Kraft Foods. Dave came to my grandmother's door every day with a selection of milk, cheese, butter — and conversation. He knew the neighborhood like nobody's business. He knew if Mrs. Grady's back was acting up again or if the Murphy boys were in trouble or how a new business on the corner was faring. He was a hub of neighborhood news. When he arrived at the door for my grandmother to examine his goods and make her selections, he'd share what he'd learned and pick up a few tidbits from her. Then, business over, he'd gather up his wares and be on his way.

Dave was a master at the art of branding, and he used conversation to make it happen. To this day the Sealtest name means quality and reliability to me. I can't put butter on my bread without hearing Dave chatting up his customers. Certainly, conversation wasn't necessary to the sale. It was pretty clear to anyone what he sold. He could simply have arrived, sold, and left. The conversation was part of cementing the brand.

As I grew my own little business, this was a lesson that came back to me — and one I tried to apply. What was so great about Dave and his product line? Was it really the taste? Did other butter taste inferior? Or would we never even have considered buying another guy's butter when we knew and did business with Dave?

In our flower shop, we always had a pot of coffee on. You didn't need coffee to sell flowers. We also had a couple of chairs in the shop — also not a requirement of the flower retail business. But I had them in there because of Dave. We brewed coffee and set up chairs as a way to invite our customers to drop by, have a cup of joe, and share with us the news of the neighborhood. You didn't have to buy anything. You didn't have to be in possession of gripping, groundbreaking revelations. Any old chat would do. The key was making time for conversation — as Dave always did — in the daily rhythm of life.

This is how we built our brand in the early days. In fact, it still is.

Conversations Solidify a Business

Sometimes, when a business starts to grow and everyone begins to think, "Hey, this might really work," it's time to remember how you got there. Often, trouble comes when entrepreneurs decide they are "grown up" enough to shed all their early entrepreneurial activities and take on the tactics of the big guys.

The truth is the tactics that got you started are the ones that will build your business into something big. And this was a challenge for us. We had grown up on conversation. But now we were growing too big to sit down and have coffee with each customer. What could we do?

For starters, we sought out partners and staff who valued conversation the way we did. This seems like such a small thing, but as we grew, we did our best to hire staff with warm, outgoing personalities. It is sometimes hard to feel warm and fuzzy in a retail transaction. There can be barriers between people — a counter or a telephone line. These can be obstacles to the human relationship. We looked for people with the skills and the desire to overcome those obstacles again and again and again.

That emotional connection is critical to the sale. We didn't see it in just our own flower shops. Consider the effect of the Walmart Greeter. This individual's job is simply to smile and greet you with warmth and emotion as you enter the store to shop. That's it. And people love it. It humanizes the vast, cavernous experience of the megastore. It makes an impersonal experience seem personal again. Most shoppers, when greeted, will smile and answer back with a "Hello" or "How are you?" It's a natural response. It's a tiny snippet of conversation that makes Walmart stand out from the discount chain crowd.

We were looking for a similar effect. If Walmart could make the vestibule of a discount store feel warm and friendly, surely we could achieve something analogous over the telephone. So while everyone else hired reps for speed, accuracy, and punctuality, we added friendliness to our wish list. We wanted our staff to sound like people you'd like to meet.

These are the conversations that ultimately build businesses into brands. Over the years, we've invested hundreds of millions of dollars into building our brand through marketing activities. If someone has a bad experience with anyone from our team — from an employee in one of our stores dealing with a customer to one of our IT folks interacting with a business partner — all of that investment is for naught. That customer or partner will forget everything good they've heard about us and remember only the bad interaction. Our brand is only as strong as our team.

So as your business grows, it becomes crucial to understand the conversations that are taking place not just in your presence but on your behalf. When it comes to your brand, who is speaking for you? Are you attracting team members who are empathetic, responsible, and considerate people willing to work hard and embrace what your brand is all about? Or are you hiring showboats and show-offs willing to say anything to get ahead?

We knew early on the importance of finding smart, motivated, energetic people who want the company to succeed. In many respects, that's what other organizations look for, too. To my mind, these are just the "table stakes" — the bare minimum that a potential employee must have in order to be successful in the workplace. On top of all that, I look for people who let you see their capacity for empathy every time they open their mouths. People who ask you how your kids are doing and actually care about the answer.

Is that unique to our business? To a business engaged in the everyday desire to express and connect? Maybe. But I'd argue that it doesn't matter whether you sell gizmos or gladioluses. If your team isn't talking to your customers, partners, and suppliers, listening and reacting to their responses, then whom are they talking to?

And what does all this talking say about your brand? Does it convey the message that yours is a business that cares? These are the conversations you need to foster throughout your organization.

We do. And like Walmart, we have found that a little warmth goes a long way. Our warmest and most friendly phone reps are our most successful. They are the voices that make our callers feel as though they are chatting with a friend rather than engaging in a retail sale.

Cultural Conversations

Often a business focuses so much on our contact with the customer that internal conversations often get short shrift. But I believe strongly in the power of culture to bind and support a company as it moves forward.

One of the ways people engage in cultural conversations is by sharing their stories. In our business, we are often involved with customers when they are engaged in life's most emotional moments — in celebration, in mourning, in love. We encourage our employees to do what's necessary to make the customer happy in these important moments in life, and that often makes for some great stories.

Here's one that everyone at 1-800-Flowers.com knows well: the story of Mrs. Williams's bouquet.

It was Mother's Day — our biggest day of the year — and we'd gotten a last-minute order to deliver a bouquet to a nursing home. We reached out to one of our florists nearby. He was just closing up for the day and was going to take a bouquet to only his own mother on his way out. But, at our request, he took this one last order, put the two bouquets in his car, and headed off for the nursing home.

When he arrived, he left his mom's bouquet in his car and took the delivery up the steps. As he entered, one of the residents, an elderly lady, called out to him, "Is that for me? Did my children send me flowers?"

"What's your name?" asked our florist. Our florist checked the card.

"Mrs. Williams."

"No, these flowers are for Mrs. Smith."

Mrs. Williams looked crestfallen. "My kids never remember me," she said.

Our florist hesitated for a split second — and then decided his own mother would understand. He delivered the first bouquet and then went back to his car for the one meant for his mother. He didn't even have to alter the card, which read "Happy Mother's Day, Mom! You're the greatest!" He went back into the nursing home and found Mrs. Williams.

"You know what, Mrs. Williams? I made a mistake and left your order in the car by accident. These are your flowers. Happy Mother's Day."

Mrs. Williams cried. Our florist cried. The staff at the nursing home cried.

So if that story involved just one florist, and perhaps a few staffers at 1-800-Flowers.com, how come everyone at the company knows it?

It's a legend. We have a book of them — stories of extraordinary customer service efforts. Along with the story of "Mrs. Williams's Bouquet," we have many other tales of team members going above and beyond to make a customer happy. We have the story about the customer service rep who fielded a furious call from a customer and calmly, sweetly handled the redelivery request — knowing all along that the customer was dead wrong and had given us the wrong address. (The customer herself realized the error later and acknowledged the rep's superior service in a letter to us.) We have the story about the World War II veteran who asked us to deliver a flower to his wartime sweetheart, whom he hadn't seen in decades. We did. (We did the flowers for the subsequent wedding, too. That's also in the legends book.)

One of my personal favorites has gone down in our company's history as "The Cop and the Rose." In addition to Mother's Day, the holiday that really revs up our operation is Valentine's Day. I was present for one of our great Valentine's Day legends as it happened.

That afternoon, I was in our service center looking for one of our supervisors. Everyone told me she was busy and had asked not to be disturbed. It took me three hours to track her down, and when I finally did, she told me what she'd been doing all that time.

"I have an order for a customer's sick aunt in a small town outside of Pittsburgh," she explained. "I've been trying to find a florist who can make the delivery in time for Valentine's Day."

It hadn't gone well. This town was just so out of the way, we could not convince a florist to take the time during this busy time of year to drive all the way out there to deliver the order.

But this supervisor — Gloria — didn't give up. She continued to call around until she reached a local police officer who also ran the town's hardware store. The officer knew the town and knew the destination. He offered to make the delivery. So Gloria — after three hours devoted to this project — had the bouquet delivered to the hardware store and the cop agreed to drive it the final few miles to Auntie.

The police officer called us the next day to relay this message from the aunt: "You didn't just make my day or my week or my month. You and my wonderful nephew made my whole year!"

All these legends fuel an ongoing internal conversation. No amount of off-site training sessions and memos from the boss can do what staffers do when they talk among themselves and share their own war stories. These conversations have power. They reinforce what we're trying to do as a company. They reward hard work with the one thing most people really crave — positive recognition for a job well done. Because we take the time to collect and distribute the legends, we ensure that the conversation is ongoing. The story of Mrs. Williams is not forgotten when new employees come onboard and those who were part of the original story have moved on. We've institutionalized our stories and made storytelling an integral part of the company.

These are the conversations that are crucially important to have as you grow your business. In the early days, when there are just a handful of employees, it's easy to swap stories during a coffee break. Everyone knows what everyone else is doing.

When a company grows, that intimacy falls away and you get into a completely different pattern of communication. The casual exchange of great stories from the trenches falls away and is replaced my memos and meetings and PowerPoint presentations. It's important as a firm expands to remember to keep the tug-at-your-heartstrings conversations alive and flowing. These are the stories that raise us up and keep us focused on the positive purpose of our lives.

Conversations for Hiring

How you staff up as your company grows is critical. Every company would like to know the secret to hiring the right people. I have a tip of my own. Not surprisingly, it is based on conversation.

This technique is based on one I developed back when I worked at the home in Queens. The boys who came to us had come from difficult circumstances, to say the least. To engage with them and to get them to buy into our rules and regulations, I developed what appeared to the boys to be an entrance interview. But it was a conversation in disguise.

I asked each new boy a series of questions about the circumstances that had brought them to the home. Were they having problems at home? At school? With drugs? With gangs? All of the boys had already been accepted and placed in the home, so there was no real hurdle to clear. But they didn't know that, and that gave me an opportunity to get them to open up and talk to me.

It was in this process that I developed a question I still use in interviews today. I often share it with managers when I talk about hiring. It is: "What am I going to see in your behavior a year from now that you'll wish you had told me today?" This is the question that heads off all kinds of problems down the line. This is where I learn that the poised, accomplished person before me has a fear of public speaking — and wants coaching and practice in that department. This is where I learn that an engineer has a hidden passion for marketing. This is where I learn an individual has family demands that may limit how long he can realistically stay with us.

Everyone likes to put their best face forward in a job interview. This is a question I use to break through the facade and get to the real personality of the applicant. It worked on the troubled boys in Queens and it works in my company as well. When you ask the right questions, people will open up. Suddenly you've moved from an interrogation to a dialogue.

Conversations to Grow

Companies evolve over time, and many moments of great change are sparked by conversation. The decision whether or not to pursue a new avenue, take on a new partner, or make a big investment is usually not made by one person. It's a collection of voices that come together to determine a company's next step.

One of our big moments of change came when we decided to do business with AOL. We were the first retailer to sign on to what was then a nascent area of business. Since e-commerce really had no track record in those days, we had to rely on something other than data and financials. This is a story I love to tell about how conversation can lead you forward in business, even when the numbers fail to persuade.

My brother Chris and I traveled down to Virginia to have lunch with Steve Case and Ted Leonsis at AOL. We four sat in a restaurant and discussed the prospect of doing business together in this undiscovered country. Steve and Ted talked technology. Chris and I couldn't understand half of what they said. And we couldn't see much of their acumen as businessmen either. When the meal ended, our hosts didn't have enough cash on hand to cover the check and we all had to pitch in to avoid doing dishes.

But before we left the restaurant, Chris and I stepped aside to compare notes. We didn't really get all the technological elements

Steve and Ted had going. And we could tell they didn't have a ton of cash. Yet both Chris and I sensed something in them — something that didn't show in the financials or the paperwork, but came through in conversation. We could see their passion. We could see they had a vision for where they were going and that we could be a part of the journey.

We went back to the table — back to the two guys who talked tech-speak and didn't have enough cash to cover a lunch bill — and said yes. It was a key juncture for 1-800-Flowers — a moment when we committed to being a part of the impending digital revolution.

Conversations to Shrug Off

There are some conversations that are best left ignored. Well, if not ignored, then at least marginalized. These are the conversations that you can't avoid, but that you shouldn't allow to get you down. When I find myself in them, I make a mental note to move on. These are usually conversations in which the other guy is throwing around the word "never."

"Gas prices will never go over four dollars!"

"People will never pay more for organic groceries!"

"People will never shop online!"

If there's one word that inspires me to work harder, push further, and dream bigger, it's the word "never."

There have been too many times during my personal and professional life when critics have told me that something would never work: You'll never make a profit. That will never fly. You'll never be able to grow hair like Cher.

OK, that last one was true. But the other "nevers" are just negative vibes standing in the way of true innovation.

When I hear "never" in conversation, I actually find it a bit inspirational. It's a challenge. As a student of business innovation, I know that the word "never" has inspired many to leap forward, Edison, Bell, Gates, Buffett (both Warren and Jimmy), and Steve Jobs among them. Here's a famous internal memo from Western Union in 1878: "This 'telephone' has too many shortcomings to be seriously considered as a means of communication. The device is inherently of no value to us."

Here's a comment made by Darryl Zanuck, head of Twentieth Century Fox, in 1946: "Television won't be able to hold on to any market it captures after the first six months. People will soon get tired of staring at a plywood box every night."

Creators of something new and different often hear the phrase "That will never work."

Here's my advice: When you hear "nevers," don't waste your time trying to change people's minds. They are naysayers. These are conversations that can't help you. Remember that for every voice that said, "Nah, that can never happen," there was someone with ingenuity, creativity, and drive who said, "Well, maybe so, but I'm going to try anyway."

If we, the entrepreneurs, were willing to listen to the negative, we would have given up long ago. We would have accepted the idea that there is nothing else new to create, no place left to explore. To start and build a business, you have to be the one who knows better. You have to smile politely at the "nevers" and reach out to other people. Ask questions, look for solutions, try new ideas, form alliances. "Never" is a word you hear a lot; don't take it as a sentence. Take it as a challenge.

When to Shut Up

Finally, in the process of starting and building a business, there are the conversations you don't have.

As a boss, you have to remember that anything you say may have an unintended ripple effect. Sometimes, that's for the good. You speak about an important topic and the word goes out throughout the company that it's something you care about and want to see addressed. But sometimes, the ripple that is generated can lead in an unproductive direction.

For that reason, I've learned to keep some conversations in my head. I was touring a shop once, and as I looked around, I could see there were some things that I would have done differently. Little things. I looked around at the trash buckets and thought, "You know, they would be a lot easier to empty and keep clean if they were lined with a trash bag first." But I held my tongue. Even a stray comment from me about something as innocuous as trash bags can have unintended consequences. So I've learned to let these things go.

I was slow to pick up on this lesson as a one-man band evolving into a business executive. In the early days of my company's growth spurt, I still wanted to do it all. I simply tried to get by on less sleep. That worked for a while, but one day I was so tired the flight crew on my plane to Dallas could barely rouse me on landing. Although I got off the plane under my own power that day, it was dawning on me that this "do it all" methodology wasn't sustainable. Part of growing as a company is growing as a leader and learning new ways to communicate effectively with the emerging network of talent you've amassed.

Leaders in Conversation: Conversations with Norman

When I began my career as a retailer, I kept my job as a counselor at the boys' home. Little did I know that the home would foster my careerlong exploration of conversation as a leadership tool. It was there that I made the discovery that would propel my entire business career: In order to move forward with anyone or anything, first you have to connect.

There was one particularly hard case at the home, a young man named Norman. A story I often tell about Norman revolves around the one day I decided to make my mother happy and take some of her seedling tomato plants out to the home. I was busy digging up an inhospitable patch of the backyard when Norman came by and asked me what I was doing.

"Planting tomatoes," I told him.

He quickly shot back that pot would be a more useful crop, and besides, the plants would be torn up by someone in the neighborhood soon enough. I shrugged and kept at my gardening.

Norman was clearly intrigued. After a while, he started handing me my gardening tools. Finally, he asked if he could plant a seedling himself. I made a big deal out of deciding whether he was ready for that level of responsibility.

Over those scraggly tomato plants, on that sandy bit of ground that was more driveway than garden, we connected.

Every day, Norman was there to help me weed, water, and tend to these plants. And during these periods together, we talked. About football, about school, about whatever was on his mind. It didn't really matter. The conversational portal between us had been opened. It was an eye-opening experience for me and one that I have carried into my life and my business since that day. It doesn't matter how important or engaging your information is — to get it across to the other person, first you have to connect. Once you connect, the conversation can begin.

What happened to Norman? It's hard to say. Some of the boys from the home stayed in touch with me. Others cropped up in my life quite unexpectedly later on — with tales of success and jobs and family. I was always happy to see that. Some went out into the world and I never heard from them again. But I knew that they moved forward having connected with me. Norman helped me learn to do that.

AFTER WORDS: TAKE NOTE

One of the biggest mistakes people make is relying on memory to store the important details after a conversation is over. I've learned over the years that memory is unreliable. Throughout the day, and certainly after an engaging conversation, I make notes. I make them on the paper I keep in my pocket, on agendas from meetings, and on my smartphone. I make sure to record whatever happened so that I can build upon that information later.

My note-taking process may look casual on the surface, but I have honed it over the years so that I can do it without thinking. I keep my tools at hand at all times — in fact, in the early days of my company I was known for always having two felt-tipped pens clipped to my shirt.

(I have since traded those in for a higher class of writing instrument.) I make note taking an ongoing part of my day, and finish each day by making sure the information is filed away for future use.

NEXT STEP: GET OUT

In the early years of my company, I spent about half of each year on the road. This was an obvious imperative as I sought to build things and create a sense of momentum, but I have continued the process of travel long after many other leaders would consider it necessary. I leave my office for the road because that's where conversation happens.

I have hired and trained a dynamic team of executives. We have embraced a range of impressive technological tools (and I try them all myself). Nothing, in my experience, is as powerful as the face-to-face meeting. Nothing inspires people to do their best and share their most ambitious efforts more than the moment when they see the boss, shake his hand, and hear him say: "Tell me what you're working on." This is what I remind myself when I'm sitting on the tarmac at Kennedy or O'Hare or LAX, tenth in line for takeoff. Once you get to the corner office, you need to realize that the best conversations take place far away from it.

McCANN'S PRINCIPLE NUMBER ONE: CONVERSE — EVEN IF YOU THINK YOU CAN'T

You don't need an innate gift of gab. Conversation leadership can be learned and practiced. Even if you're shy, begin conversations and hang in there to see them through. Practice will build your confidence, and over time, you'll begin to see your own value in the conversation process.

2

—

Conversation Management

T HE SAYING GOES: It's lonely at the top. This is the image many of us carry as we move through the business world. Leadership is often understood as going it alone: sitting in your office, tilting back in your leather chair, and pondering the hard decisions the boss must make. However, this is an antiquated version of leadership, and certainly not one that I recommend. If I had to sit in my office alone all day, I'd have returned to bartending a long time ago.

My time at work is actually spent anywhere but in my own office. I pop in and out of all corners of the building. I drop by my managers' offices and by our team members' offices. I am on the road quite a bit, but during my days at headquarters, it's no use stopping by my office to find me. You'd be better off standing in a hallway, because chances are I will walk right by you.

My walkabout style is not just one that keeps me entertained. It is part of my leadership process, integral to the concept of conversation leadership. You can't have a truly great conversation alone in your office no matter how good the technology (the telephone, e-mail, instant messaging, Skype). All of these fall short of the best kind of conversation, which is a face-to-face exchange.

In this chapter, I'll cover the ways I've found conversation leadership to be helpful not only in the "big picture" projects a business might take on, but also in the day-to-day workplace experience. Conversation can be more than just a high-level leadership tool; it can also be a ground-level management tool. I define "conversation management" as a subset of conversation leadership. It is the use of conversation as a management tool in the everyday working process — not in meetings or in strategy sessions but in the everyday interactions that take place in a business.

The practice of conversation management is not well taught in business schools or, quite frankly, in most businesses. It is commonly accepted that leaders must be decisive and deliver orders with confidence and clarity. I am not against clarity, but I do think that the opportunity to manage employees in a conversational process is often overlooked in favor of clear and confident proclamations. In the daily grind of getting the job done, using conversation to manage can pay dividends for everyone in the organization — from hourly employees to the C-suite. In this chapter, I'll detail the different ways conversation management can be deployed.

One-on-One

A few years back, in the early days of social networking, I e-mailed a memo to a wide group of tech staff in the company. The memo reviewed some new developments in the online communication world and contained some of my thoughts on where things might be headed in the future. I hit "send" and prepared to move on to other tasks of the day.

Within about five minutes, a return e-mail landed in my in box. A relatively new employee in my technology department had sent my memo back to me — with corrections. Many, many corrections. The memo was marked up with comments, suggestions, and references to other sources of information on the topic. He had torn my memo to pieces.

For many corporate leaders, this would mark the end of the story (and possibly that employee's career). This type of exchange, however, is a platform for continued conversation. Since the responder and I were both in the same building, I took the opportunity to step away from the keyboard and track him down.

I found the employee working at his cubicle and walked right up to him.

"How dare you?" I thundered.

The man's eyes popped wide as he wondered whether he was about to get fired for challenging the boss. I quickly put my arm around his shoulder to let him know I was kidding, and sat down.

"Tell me more about this," I said. "Show me these references. Talk to me about what else is going on here."

That started the conversation. We talked most specifically about Facebook — how it was not just a toy for young people, but also a tool with substantial business potential. From there, we talked about the effect of social networking on business and how that platform was becoming more influential in the way customers make decisions. Finally, we brought it back to our own company and discussed what Facebook might mean for the business one day. That conversation was the first of many in which this employee would participate and lead as we began a more aggressive effort in experimenting with social networking.

This is a classic example of what I try to promote in my company and in my advice to others in the business world: You can harness conversation not only to exchange viewpoints but also to move forward and make progress. By engaging this individual in conversation, I not only led him to understand how his input was needed and valued, I also modeled for him a conversation method I then watched him carry forward independently.

How did all of this happen in one conversation?

Use of humor

When I walked up and delivered my "How dare you?" line, I did it with forethought. This is a tactic I use often. I play the disgruntled boss, pretending to be dismayed with an employee's performance. I've done this enough around the office that everyone who works here knows I'm kidding. I'm not such a great actor that if you heard me do this, you'd be completely fooled. Usually a new employee, hearing me deliver my lines for the first time, has a moment of panic. *Oh, no! Is he really angry?* It's quickly apparent that I'm not, and everyone has a little chuckle at the ruse. The relief following a little shock like this paves the way for a lighter, more honest relationship.

Humor is a tremendous conversation starter. Much the same way a speaker will open with a joke, I open with a moment of play-acting. When you get someone to smile, even laugh, you allow emotions to rise up to the surface. That is the perfect moment to engage in conversation. You have opened a pathway between yourself and the other individual, and you've begun a connection of warmth and fellowship.

Many people quake when they see the boss coming or sense a difficult conversation approaching. When I bring a little bit of humor to the moment, I break down that natural panic and replace it with a moment of emotional connection. When I then reach out to continue the conversation, it's one in which both parties are already smiling. It is my way of setting up an authentic exchange of ideas, rather than polite and meaningless chatter. I've found that the smile itself produces a chain reaction. If I'm smiling and I can provoke another person to smile, that exchange is going to open our minds and set us both up for a genuine connection. Smiling softens your "game face" for a moment, and in that opening there's often an opportunity to make a conversation a moment of actual progress rather than just one of the many chance encounters of a day at the office.

Of course, humor is not 100 percent foolproof. I have had occasions where my use of humor went over like a lead balloon. I was recently doing business in a European country known for its emotional reserve and cool demeanor. My hosts just weren't sure what to do with me. By the end of the trip, they'd gotten to know me well enough that they were able to recognize my humor — even though they may still have been somewhat baffled by it. I find that 90 percent of the time, a small dose of (office-appropriate) humor works beautifully. In the business world, we are so concerned about our image that we forget to foster and value emotional bonds. Use the old etiquette yardstick of avoiding politics and religion and keep your humor inclusive rather than exclusive, diminishing of others. But if it's a question of not having a conversation at all, or trying out a joke that might bomb, always try the joke. Even if humor falls flat, it still invites a response.

Choice of location

I did not invite the memo writer to "step into my office," even though asking him to do so would have been a perfectly reasonable way for us to have this conversation. I could have even used my "How dare you?" in that setting. I chose not to do this because inviting the individual into an office cuts down on one of the key benefits of conversation leadership for managers: the eavesdroppers.

You can bet that everyone in a five-desk radius saw me coming that afternoon. I don't slip quietly through the halls of my company. I'm a pretty visible guy. By the time I reached the cubicle of my memo writer, I had an audience. I knew that; it's a part of my process.

Everyone in the immediate area saw me joke with the memo writer and pull up a chair to have an extended conversation with him about the advent of social networking. By having this conversation in such a visible venue, I did more than converse with one employee; I let everyone in earshot know how I manage and what I want from them as employees of the company. I telegraphed my interest in the topic and my desire to talk with people about it. I was open to that conversation, I was eager to have it, and I was willing to schlep around to find the person who would have it with me. My conversation with this employee had the potential to resonate with a wider group. Behind a closed door, it could not have had that impact.

I do this often — not just to educate new employees, but also to set an ongoing cultural tone for the company. We are a business that values the frank exchange of ideas. We are not a firm that stands on ceremony or hierarchy. We want to hear from each other and learn from each other, to keep the lines of communication open and flowing. This is a hallmark of our organization. By choosing a public location for my conversations, I reinforce this as a core theme of our company culture.

The art of the drop-by

Suppose I'd responded to the edited memo by scheduling a meeting: an individual meeting with the writer, or maybe even a team meeting with a larger group to discuss the writer's points. This would have been a good way to process the information I'd received, but it would also have set a poor example for everyone in the company. I don't want to be the only one engaged in conversation management. My process is designed to inspire my staff to converse with me and with one another, at any time. I do what I can to reduce the barriers to conversation with me; beyond that, I try to model the behavior I want to see in others.

Whenever I'm aware that there's someone in the building with something interesting to say, I drop by to have a conversation with that person. Conversation should not be a stilted or heavily regulated process. It should happen at the drop of a hat, without warning. My impromptu visit modeled what I hope other staffers will copy — the art of the drop-by. The more conversations you have, the more likely you are to generate moments of conversation leadership; therefore, conversations must be daily, commonplace events.

Managing a Group

Conversation management is a tool that has many uses. While it may seem like a process best used one-on-one, I've found that a conversation management approach can be very effective when working with a group. It's not the easiest conversation process to manage, and it requires some setup and tactical skill. Some things to keep in mind:

- Be convincing in your initial pitch and patient enough to wait for the response. Groups respond more slowly than individuals.
- Set up a structure that is easily accessible by all, so that the group can converse with you and with each other.
- Take the long view, and communicate that to the group so that everyone knows the conversation will be ongoing.

It's labor-intensive, but when conversation engages a group, the results are often dramatic. Done well, a manager can inspire a group to move forward with his or her message and mission in mind.

I recently traveled to a Midwest market in which we do business and met with a group of about twenty-five employees for dinner. They ranged from top local managers to newcomers to the company, and the location was a lovely suburban Italian restaurant.

We gathered at the bar as everyone arrived, and I moved around the room, meeting and greeting. I introduced one newcomer to a veteran of my company. As we picked up our drinks and began to move to the dining room, I heard the veteran say to the newcomer: "Are you ready to sing for your supper?"

She replied, "What's that?"

She soon found out. When I hold a dinner (which I do routinely), I spend the meal engaging the group in conversation. This is not just the idle chitchat of coworkers spending an evening out, although that is part of it. My mission at any dinner is to inspire the group to partake in the kind of meaningful conversation in which great ideas are born.

This night was no exception. I let the ordering proceed, then began the conversation. I spoke for a minute myself, talking about an issue or two from the main office that would be of interest to the local market — how the latest numbers from our financial performance had been received, plans for our run-up to an important holiday sales season, and so forth. Then I began to choose speakers. I started with experienced managers — those who had been to my dinners before and were prepared. I listened, asked questions, and looked for ways to build on what was being said. Then I made sure to hear from others. There are always one or two who aren't sure they want to participate in the conversation. Perhaps they are new to the company, or they are just naturally shy. I make a particular effort to call on those individuals to speak. The message to the table is consistent: everyone has something to contribute to this gathering.

On a good night, the conversation will take on its own momentum. Speakers will spark ideas in one another; colleagues will make new connections, see new opportunities, and make plans to continue the conversation back at the office. They'll be inspired to continue the momentum even after I've left the table.

The conversation will often get away from me as speakers jump in and begin to drive their own momentum. I love when this happens. It's great fun to see a conversation take off.

In other situations, conversation management is not as easy. On that same Midwest trip, I addressed a group of store managers at their annual meeting. This was not an ideal conversation environment. First of all, I was the third speaker. The group had already been sitting there, watching two different PowerPoint presentations in a row. What's more, the room was set up auditorium-style and I was at the front, holding a microphone, addressing an audience arranged in rows to face me.

It didn't look like a conversation. It looked like a lecture. Who wants to have a conversation in a lecture hall?

I opened with humor. I made a few quick remarks about my New Yawk accent — something every Midwesterner in the room had already noticed, but I gave them permission to chuckle a bit. I threw in a joke about my old neighborhood in Queens and the relative likelihood that some of my childhood pals now share an office with Tony Soprano. I chipped away at the facade my title and my place at the front of the room naturally created. Now those in the audience were closer to a place where they could consider having a real conversation with me.

I used my time to impart some key information I knew the store managers needed to know about our work back at headquarters. Then I moved into the conversational phase of my presentation.

"I want to connect with this community," I told them. "This is a dialogue we are beginning today. I need you to begin a conversation with me. I need your ideas. I need to hear what you think. You need to hear what your fellow store managers think. We need to have this conversation."

I must have used the word "conversation" a dozen times — and that was necessary. This was not a one-on-one meeting. This was not even one of my "sing for your supper" dinner parties. This was a captive audience at a business presentation. In order for this to be the start of a conversation, I was going to have to lead them there. Sometimes, when you address an audience and invite them to converse with you, they pop their hands in the air and demand the microphone. The results are inspiring. More often, though, they don't move. To lead this kind of group forward, you have to be convincing in your original pitch and patient enough to wait for the results to come in; then, respond accordingly.

One of the steps I took that day was to invite the group to continue the conversation with me via a company blog. This gave the store managers a framework in which they could take me up on my offer of an idea exchange. In a one-on-one exchange, there are moments when you must remember to stop talking and listen. When conversing with a group, you have to create an easily accessible structure to ensure that others have a way to respond to you and each other.

And as I mentioned, a key ingredient to using conversation in a group setting is a promise to continue the exchange. I met recently with a work group in our headquarters — a team that was small enough to fit in a conference room. I began by asking the following questions: What could we be doing to improve results in this group? How can we generate great new ideas and help them

31

become a reality? What needs to happen in this group to propel it forward?

The meeting went well, but the most important technique of conversation management appeared in only its final moments: I promised that group we would be back soon, in this same conference room, eating these same lousy tuna sandwiches, continuing this same conversation. It's the knowledge that the dialogue will continue that inspires those you manage to take what you say back to their desks and to think about what to do next.

The best way to set the stage for this continued dialogue is to let the group know that this will be a two-way street. Make it clear that you are there to speak *and* to listen. Emphasize that you'll be asking questions and expecting answers, now and in the ongoing dialogue that will continue past the meeting. It's like telling a classroom full of students, "This will be on the test." Once you announce to a group that you expect interactivity, not passivity, you help reset their brains. When people find themselves in a situation in which they'll be asked to recall information, they listen differently. The same is true when audience members know that when you're done speaking, it will be their turn.

Manager-to-Manager

One of the most challenging areas in which to use conversation leadership as a management tool is when dealing with managers. These can be difficult encounters; I may be communicating my displeasure about something or telling an individual something he doesn't want to hear. When you're dealing with management-level individuals, prepare to be engaged. That person may not simply take what you're saying, go back to his or her desk, and try to do a better job. You may be in for more of an argument. The stakes may be high — there may be a lot of money in play, a new venture at stake, or jobs on the line. My encounter with my technology memo writer allowed me to leverage my more senior status; when I deal with managers, I am closer to being on equal footing. I'm still the boss, but there is less of a gulf between us in terms of hierarchy.

One of the ways I handle a management conversation is by conducting a dress rehearsal. Cast opposite me in this play is, more times than not, my brother Chris. Chris and I did not grow up together; he was only seven years old when I went off to college. The relationship we've developed over the years has been very much connected to our relationship in the workplace. We have less of the rivalry you might expect among brothers in a business. He is often my first stop when I'm getting ready to have a challenging manager-to-manager conversation.

Recently, I prepped for a conversation that I knew would not be enjoyable — one in which I would express my concerns over recent events. I ran through it with Chris first, completely unfiltered. I said everything I wanted to say, expressing all my emotions, disappointments, and general complaints. Then we went over the conversation together, taking it apart and creating a new framework. I asked myself, What do I want to achieve with this conversation? How can I resolve matters to bring about the result I want? What is my best guess as to the real motivations of this manager? By conducting a dress rehearsal, I was able to expunge all my emotions on the topic — all the elements that might have inflamed the situation further. I was prepared to bring only what was useful to the real conversation with the manager in question.

Through these dry runs, I am able to place a safety valve on my emotions. There are plenty of people who bypass this process, who go through life without a filter. They blast their views uncensored, and, in my opinion, they miss opportunities to resolve situations more peacefully and effectively.

There are times when a conversation with a manager has to happen over time, rather than in one sitting. One series of discussions I had with Chris took place over the course of several months. A manager at our company was not working out. I could see that ultimately the best solution would be for Chris to step back into that particular role and reset the course. Rather than deliver this as an order, I approached the situation as a conversation that unfolded over time. Chris and I discussed this problem and its potential solutions many times, and each time I would drop bread crumbs, pressing him: What do you think needs to be done here? What is our best solution? Eventually, he came to see what I did: that the situation required his hands-on attention. Perhaps this wasn't a traditional conversation; it was more like an evolution in thinking. It was a solution reached via conversation, using the connection and the exchange of ideas to move us forward.

Certainly it was not the fastest way to communicate to Chris what I hoped would happen, but in the long run it was the most efficient. An order may be carried out quickly — but is everyone convinced that it's the best solution? With conversation leadership, the process is slower, but the payoff is more solidified. At the end of our series of conversations, Chris and I were both convinced that the decision to move that problem manager out of the job was the right one. When it happened, there was no hesitancy. We had talked it through; the angles were all covered.

The Difficult Conversation

If you're going to run a business, someday you'll have to fire someone.

It's a very hard conversation to have. Even if you've had it many times and are very experienced, it's still stressful. I find it particularly painful to tell someone that I no longer want him or her working with me. I always hire people with a sense of anticipation and promise. When it doesn't work out as I'd planned, I feel the loss for myself and for the company.

But what I've learned over the years is that this particular conversation does not require or even really benefit from my emotions. In fact, it's a conversation that needs some very specific and often overlooked elements. The difficult conversation — the one that conveys "You're fired" — needs two things: clarity and structure.

Jack Welch gave me a quick lesson on the first. The man who early on earned the nickname "Neutron Jack" never seemed to shy away from firing anyone. I often tell the story of the time I encountered him at a cocktail hour. He told me that the best thing to do when you know that someone needs to be fired is to fire them. Fast. It is the hesitation — the impetus to avoid the difficult conversation — that makes everything worse for everyone. I shared with him that Chris and I were having difficulty making what we had already decided was a necessary cut in our executive staff. Jack actually grabbed me by the jacket lapels as he delivered this advice.

"Jim, have you ever heard someone say, 'I wish we'd waited six more months to fire that bastard'?"

So Jack was able to help us see that part of the process. When you want to fire someone, don't hesitate and hope the conversation won't have to happen. Act with clarity of purpose.

But the grab-the-guy-by-the-lapels strategy wasn't exactly my style, and my brother and I needed more advice to help these conversations go more smoothly. For that, we turned to Jim Cannavino, a member of our board and a longtime executive at IBM. IBM is a big company and no stranger to layoffs and other difficult conversations. Jim shared with us a management process that makes even difficult conversations go more smoothly.

The key, he told us, is to create a structure of feedback from manager to employee — one that constantly communicates how things are going and how well everyone is meeting expectations. At IBM, this was sorted into three familiar categories: Red, Yellow, Green. As an employee, you knew on what color block you stood at any given time. Establishing that status made any conversation about performance — even a difficult one — less complicated. The structure of the system made the conversation easier on both parties. It certainly helped Chris and me as we created a means to talk about what to do when things aren't working out.

Conversation management is a style that requires practice, and I find it requires consistent explanation. Every new individual who joins my company may end up engaged in a conversation with me, and not all of them will be used to the practice. For most people, this was not how business was done at the old job. When the boss spoke, you listened and nodded. Since that is not the way I want to manage, I find that it is helpful to see myself as a mentor of the conversation leadership process. To consistently engage in this type of management, I must routinely explain it, model it, and teach it to new managers so they can bring it out to a wider array of employees. When we all partake in conversation leadership and conversation management, the payoff to the company at large couldn't be clearer.

LEADERS IN CONVERSATION: MEET THE NEW BOSS

There was a new employee working in our headquarters. I spotted her as I made my way back to my office one day, so I stopped by her desk.

"You must be the new employee giving your supervisor all this trouble!"

She registered a moment of shock. I was the boss! What did this mean? I made sure I was smiling so she could see quickly that I was kidding.

The new employee worked in a cubicle on an aisle, and her supervisor sat right across the walkway. The supervisor was quick to jump in.

"Oh, no, Jim, she's doing great."

I turned back to the new employee.

"So, tell me about yourself. Where are you from?"

In a few short minutes, we'd had our first conversation. It had a bit of humor, a bit of the traditional résumé recitation everyone goes through at a new job, and it sent a clear message to the new employee: I'm an approachable boss. Talk to me.

For this employee, the results were significant. She began her time at the company as a shy individual, and in the three years she's been with us, she's grown, expanded her outlook, stepped up, and really contributed. I saw recently that she was part of a team that worked on a blogger event for us, meeting and interacting with the community that covers our company online.

I've had that same basic conversation with hundreds of new employees throughout my time as a manager. It's my favorite icebreaker.

After that kind of encounter, no one is afraid to have a conversation with me.

AFTER WORDS: NAMING NAMES

Often what comes out of a conversation is not a plan or an idea, but the right words. Words that capture a vision. When you can hear the right words, secure them and begin using them with others. This is your opportunity to take elements of conversation and leverage them as leadership moments.

I had a conversation in Austin with a leading technologist. In our exchange, he said: "You're not looking to expand e-commerce. You're looking to move from e-commerce into social commerce." The words "social commerce" stuck with me, and it was this naming of the idea that gave me the vocabulary to carry back to my team and execute the evolution I was looking for in my business.

Naming can be inspirational in the face of great challenges. I have observed Joe Plumeri, the former CEO of Willis, Inc., rally his team to face dire problems in their industry by tagging the problems as "headwinds." By giving a name to the situation, he gave his team a shortcut—a way to acknowledge the hurdles to success without listing them in each conversation. The word was chosen well; it concisely described the difficult outside forces that were at work. This executive used vocabulary to focus his team.

Great politicians use this tactic when they are able to seize on a word (such as Barack Obama's "Change") that resonates with voters.

Naming is not easy. It can take time, effort, and many hours of conversation to find the name that fits the mission. For many years, I tried to inspire my team to get behind my vision for Celebrations, a new concept for the flowers business. It was difficult to achieve buy-in for what I believed was going to be our next great platform. When I heard the phrase "social commerce," I knew I'd found a name for my goal. I came back to the office using it, and instead of blank stares, I started to see glimmers of recognition. That's the power of a name.

NEXT STEPS: SET THE NEXT MEETING

I never end a meeting with "thank you" or "good-bye." I always end with the time and place of the next meeting. This puts everyone on notice that we did not have just a simple meeting, we had a conversation, and one that will continue at the next gathering.

McCANN'S PRINCIPLE NUMBER TWO: CONVERSE ACROSS HIERARCHIES

Step out of your zone. Talk to people above and below you and integrate what you learn into your peer conversations.

3
—

Conversations with Customers

WHEN YOU ARE IN the flowers business, everyone you meet is a potential customer. The stranger on the bus, the new neighbor, the potential vendor — all may one day be in the market for flowers. It's not as though we sell wind turbines or radioactive isotopes. We sell a product that most people will someday want to purchase: A sweetheart rose. A client thank-you. A Christmas wreath. Ours is a broad business. So it's no exaggeration when I say that everyone is a customer. Really, everyone is.

This fact of life does make it somewhat complicated to focus in on the topic of customer conversations. If everyone is a customer — and I've just argued that's the case — how can I give advice on how to converse with the entire population?

The truth is, "customer conversations" is a broad heading that hovers over several different kinds of interactions. Not all customer conversations are handled the same way, use the same tools, or have the same goals in mind. For the purposes of our discussion here, I'll break down the vast landscape of customer conversations into three key categories:

- Customer service conversations
- Marketing conversations
- Research conversations

In all three engagements, I am conversing with customers. But the way I do this and the results I reap are quite different in each, and they deserve individual attention.

Customer Service Conversations

"The customer is always right."

Wrong.

The customer is often incorrect. One holiday season, one of our customers took to social media to complain at length that the flowers he had ordered from us had failed to arrive at his mother's door. He wasn't shy about calling us all kinds of names. Our customer service team scrambled to find out what had gone wrong.

It turned out he'd ordered from one of our competitors. We think we have a pretty memorable name, but I guess sometimes customers get confused.

In another instance, we were the vendor of flowers for a funeral—a terrible tragedy in which several members of one family were killed in a house fire. The surviving relative kicked up a media storm when he made public his dismay that the flowers he'd ordered from us had not been delivered. Shocked, we sent a representative to the funeral home to investigate. The flowers were there.

These customers were not right. And that happens a lot. The world is full of busy people and sometimes they make mistakes. That being the case, what can we do with the adage "the customer is always right"? It's a core mantra of the modern business era. Goodness knows, our customers are familiar with it, and sometimes they recite it to us when they call. We may not think it's true, but it's part of the fabric of customer-retailer relations. This is something I learned from retail legend Stew Leonard's.

Here's what I tell our customer service teams: The customer may not always be right. But he's always the customer. When you find yourself in conversation with a customer, your job is not to accept that he's right; your job is to make him happy. Whether he's right or wrong, that's your goal.

To make that happen, we approach our training and customer service process a little differently than most. It is, like many of our efforts, rooted in the importance we place on conversation.

It starts with our training materials. Remember our Legends book? When customer service agents join us, we give them that book to read. It's not a book of scripts as you'd find in many other firms like ours. These are the stories of 1-800-Flowers.com employees who went above and beyond to make a customer happy. We tell new employees that there are no rules to our customer service process. Just read this book. If you are not performing service worthy of being in this book, you are not doing enough.

To make that possible, we free our customer service team from many of the restrictions placed on their counterparts at other firms. For one thing, we don't care how long you need to be on the phone with a customer. This is a huge break with customer service best practices — any good consulting firm will tell you that phone reps should speed through any call, dispense with that complaining voice on the other end as quickly as possible, and not dillydally with chitchat. Time is money.

We take the opposite view. In our eyes, time on the phone with a customer is golden. It's a conversation — and we do more than tolerate it. We encourage it. Our employees are empowered to stay on the phone and engage with a customer. Listen — what is the customer trying to communicate? Talk back — and not with scripted lines, but in your own voice.

That type of conversation pays dividends over and over. Here's an example we like to share: We had a high-profile business consultant address one of our franchise conventions. She was there at our invitation to speak to our franchisees about a finance topic. But she opened her remarks with a story about an experience she'd had as a 1-800-Flowers.com customer. (Remember what I said earlier? Everyone is a customer. Everyone.)

She had ordered flowers to be delivered to a family that had suffered a loss. But the flowers did not arrive as ordered. Upset, our consultant said she had called 1-800-Flowers.com and vented to the person who answered the phone.

"I was flipping out," the consultant recalled. When she paused to take a breath, the Flowers employee on the other end spoke up: "Oh, you are kidding me! Did we do that? That is terrible."

The consultant was floored. The last thing she'd expected was a sympathetic voice. She and the customer service rep then spent five minutes commiserating before agreeing on a solution.

"It was five minutes," the consultant recalled. "Five minutes on the phone, expressing sympathy, listening to me. At the end of the call, I apologized for yelling."

How might that exchange have played out if we'd been timing that customer service rep? If our instructions were for her to hurry, read the script, close the call, and move on to the next one? Speed is considered a virtue in the retail industry — it's held up as the path to profitability. But we tell our customer service employees to choose conversation over speed. It's what sets us apart from the other guys.

Over the years, we have learned some things about the art of the customer service conversation.

Cut to the chase

In the old days, we might spend hours trying to track down what had gone wrong with an angry customer's order. I had an epiphany one night just before Valentine's Day: the whole research process was a waste of time. We used to do it to ensure that people who called us with problems were really our customers — not someone trying to get over on us by calling up and demanding our help when they'd never actually ordered anything. That night before Valentine's Day, we faced the usual big spike in customer issues and a long night of chasing them down.

"Skip the research," I declared. "Don't tell the customers you'll check it out and get back to them. Just fast-forward to "'How would you like this resolved?'"

"But Jim," one of my colleagues objected, "won't that encourage people to just call us up and lie? If we don't investigate, how will we know if it's really our fault or if someone is just trying to get a free bouquet out of us?"

This was a fair point. But I stuck to my original instruction. Sure, perhaps a few bad apples will get one over on us and get free flowers because we didn't investigate first. But many more customers will be made happy by what they hear on the phone — right then and there — without waiting.

Technology amplifies a customer conversation

Whenever you bring technology into the customer conversation, the potential for it to get hot in a hurry goes way up. Technology, it seems, loosens our sharp tongues and makes us more likely to communicate harshly than we would have were we face-to-face.

When I worked in my first flower shop in Manhattan, it was unusual for someone to walk into my shop and really let me have it. Certainly, there were difficult conversations that happened, as they do in any retail business. But a true voices-raised exchange was never the norm in the store. On the phone, people were far more inclined to yell. Somehow, not having to look me in the eye made that easier. Today, in the era of digital communication, that tendency to let technology pump up the volume is pronounced. People will say things online that they'd never dream of saying to a human being at arm's length. Name-calling, vitriol, calls for legal action, boycotts, even suggestions of violence. It's a stunning example of how human beings communicate and what outside elements can shape the tone of any conversation.

We train all our customer service contact people to recognize this human phenomenon: conversation heat escalates with each layer of technology. Be aware of how the machines may be affecting the course of the conversation. Can you get an angry Facebook poster to move to a chat window? Can the Twitter user be encouraged to move to the telephone? Remember that the customers who turn to the Internet are either very, very happy or very, very angry, and the technology adds volume — and permanence — to their words. Remember in the old days when you'd be threatened in school with an infraction landing on your "permanent record"? That's what the Internet is. We train our customer service team members to understand the technologies they use — and how that technology may impact the volume of a conversation.

This is an ongoing part of our business. We are always working to stay current on where conversations are happening in the digital space and how we can best use technology to keep our customers happy. It means never resting on any one communications platform and understanding that change in this space is constant.

Conversation means listening

This goes back to our lack of time limits for customer service employees. A good conversation requires listening — and if you want to have a positive impact, you may listen more than you speak. Consider your own personal network for a moment. Who among the people you know are the best conversationalists? While you're thinking about them, do you picture them talking or listening? The truth is, the best conversationalists are top-notch listeners.

They are the individuals who understand that talking and conversing are not the same thing. They seek at all times to keep dialogue — not just noise — going.

We have on our team today an executive who spent most of his career in the army — trying to help create lasting conversations between the U.S. armed forces and local populations in hot spots all over the world. These are delicate operations in which the wrong word or a misunderstood comment can have grave implications for peace in an entire region. Conversation isn't just a pleasantry in that business. It's a critical tool. When he joined us, fresh from his experiences in Afghanistan, one of the things he told us is an adage he'd given to all his trainees in the field: "God gave you one mouth and two ears for a reason." In important conversations, listening is twice as important as talking.

Marketing Conversations

So far, I've dealt with the most obvious type of conversation you might expect us to handle at 1-800-Flowers.com — the kind where a customer calls us up or shoots us an e-mail and we engage in dialogue either to make a sale or to resolve a problem. But that's just one of the types of conversation we engage in. By the time any customer calls us or logs on to our website, we have been conversing with him or her for quite some time. But this other conversation is more broadly dispersed. This is the conversation we have via our marketing.

Marketing is not a one-way street. Believe me, I know. Years ago, I agreed to put my face in my commercials. My mug was plastered on the side of buses all over New York City. Every person who has ever seen one of those ads has taken it as an invitation to have a conversation with me.

"Hey! I know you!"

"You're Jim McCann, the flowers man!"

"You're on a bus!"

I know.

The amazing thing is not how many people saw the ads — or how many people feel compelled to tell me they saw the ads — but what they do with that moment of recognition. It is a moment in which they feel perfectly comfortable striking up a conversation with me. Some will just shout out the recognition — but most view it as the opening of a dialogue. They'll want to tell me about an experience they had buying flowers, a story they heard about someone else buying flowers, or a business idea they've been thinking about. What they have to say to me does not follow any pattern — we all have an enormous variety of things on our minds. What strikes me over and over is how effective the ads have been in starting conversations. People talk to me because as far as they're concerned, my face on the bus opened the dialogue. They're not starting a conversation. They are responding.

As much as those ads have made my life in public a bit of a challenge, I've also learned a tremendous amount from them and from their legacy. Advertising is not a one-way medium. No form of marketing really is. When we send a message out there, we should expect the customer to talk back. It's when we recognize and respond to this desire for dialogue that our marketing efforts really take off.

It's a theme I've had in my business from the very beginning.

Back at my Manhattan store on First Avenue, I decided to do

something to increase foot traffic. We had a lot of theater people working in the store at the time, and someone came up with an idea for a *Wizard of Oz* promotion. We laid out a "yellow brick road" carpet outside the store. We dressed up one of the salesgirls as Dorothy Gale. We played the soundtrack in the store. We set up floral displays tying into the storyline.

Corny? Sure. But it worked beautifully. People came into the store beaming. They all wanted to talk to us about *The Wizard of Oz*. Their favorite characters, the first time they saw the movie, the time they dressed up as the Wicked Witch for Halloween. We didn't just put out a marketing display. We put out a marketing display and invited the customer to come in and talk to us about it. Some people made purchases immediately. Other simply soaked up the good feeling the movie invoked and came back to us another time. We had created a connection. It can be as simple as that — a short exchange about a favorite scene in a beloved movie. And like that, customer and retailer are now friends — bonded over a favorite flick.

Sometimes, a marketing effort can be launched solely as a conversation starter. We did this in our pre-dot-com days when we were looking for ways to get a national conversation started about our brand. We took the old-fashioned concept of barter to a new level, setting up an arrangement with MasterCard where we bartered our floral products in exchange for tie-in promotions. And that was just the start of the program. Pretty soon, we realized all businesses can use flowers — as gifts for clients or as prize giveaways. Our goal in this effort was to generate the question: "Who did those flowers?" We created a way to spark a conversation between two customers — generating dialogue that eventually led the business back to us.

Sometimes the conversation we generate doesn't involve us at all and simply gets customers talking to each other. This is the most powerful kind of marketing there is, and it's the hardest to create and manage — marketing by word of mouth.

It's a lesson I learned early. As a youngster, my friends and I used to flock to Kresge's — one of the neighborhood five-and-dime stores. At their lunch counter, the owners ran a powerful marketing program. Everyone who ordered an ice cream sundae had the opportunity to throw a dart at the wall of balloons behind the counter. Inside each balloon was a different price. If you hit the right balloon, you could wind up paying one penny. What a deal! Kresge's didn't have to do much to promote its ice cream in my neighborhood — we did it for them. We talked all over town about how great it would be to get an ice cream sundae for a penny at Kresge's. Who would go for ice cream anywhere else? This was word-of-mouth marketing at its best.

I see this tactic employed today by the smartest businesses. I heard recently about a glassblowing studio — not a business that gets a ton of walk-in traffic — and its word-of-mouth promotion. The business, Siyeh Glass, began running a date night program. As nice as this idea is to draw people in, it is an even better idea as a conversation starter. Now the studio wasn't just something to notice as you passed by. It became a place of connection and relationship-building. It was something to talk about.

We combined the art of marketing and conversation in our latest round of advertising. We call the program personal endorsements, and we seek them from some of the great conversation starters in the marketplace today. Our goal is not just to rack up "blurbs" that say how great we are. Anyone can do that. If you look at any consumer product's marketing materials, you may be able to find a celebrity quote or two sprinkled amid the ad campaign. That's a common consumer come-on, designed to make your subconscious decide that if you buy product A, you'll look like Brad Pitt.

We take the process of using famous folks a step further and bring them into our conversation strategy. For example, one of our personal endorsements is from Rush Limbaugh. Rush is a customer — we don't leverage endorsements from anyone who is not also a customer. And he's been a customer for a long time, so it was a natural fit when we asked him to participate in this program. Rather than plaster the Rush name on our marketing materials, we asked him to do what he does best: talk to his fans. Here's the transcript:

> RUSH: As you know, whenever we have a new sponsor on the program, we take a moment out of the programming content portion to welcome the new sponsor. And this one, as is the case with all of them, we are thrilled to have. I met on Thursday afternoon last week with the CEO and the family, actually, that runs the biggest flower delivery operation in the country. They own floral shops, flower shops, they are the biggest distributors. It's 1-800-Flowers.com. And they are without question the absolute biggest in this business. They have been at it longer than anybody, and they do it better than anybody. They've got prices better than anybody, and they have a wider selection than anybody else in this business, and their prices can't be beat. It's a combination made to order for the EIB Network.

Now, those of you watching the Dittocam right now, I have a display here that is one of theirs for the holidays. They sent this to me. We just got it this morning, and it's white carnations in the shape of a little dog face complete with glasses and a Santa Claus hat. Those are white carnations that you see there. It's cute, and it's beautiful. Smells great. It's a nice holiday gift and display, particularly when you can't be somewhere for Christmas and you want to have some representation. It's a great gift, but they are simply the best at what they do, and we could not be more thrilled than to have them now be official members of the EIB family. It's 1-800-Flowers.com. It's a great website and just a tremendous system for getting you what you want, when you want it, as soon as you want it. They just can't be beat. So please welcome them. If flowers are in your immediate need, if you need any kind of arrangement for any reason, check 1-800-Flowers .com before you do anything else.

We started a powerful conversation between Rush and his audience that does more than any single ad we could buy.

Ultimately, as we've embraced the power of conversation in our marketing, our efforts to generate this type of dialogue have become more robust. One of my favorites evolved one January as we looked for ways to jump-start a strong Valentine's Day season. We called it the "Hand Us a Line for Valentine's" sweepstakes. We asked millions of customers via e-mail to submit a unique greeting card message. The winning entrant, as selected by a panel of celebrity judges, would receive a trip to the Bahamas.

The response was spectacular. Customers eagerly sent in their best ideas. We came up with a great celebrity judge panel — Willie Nelson, Jim Brickman, and Martha McBride. Our winner got a phone call from Willie Nelson telling her she'd won the vacation prize. We've continued the program for years; today, tens of thousands of customers enter every contest. Why? Well, everyone likes to win a prize, so that's one reason. But there are lots of sweepstakes out there to enter — why ours? The reason, I maintain, is the invitation to conversation. We don't just say send us your name, we'll do a drawing, and someone lucky goes on vacation. Instead, we invite customers to talk to us. Tell us a great line you've come up with, share it with us, share it with everyone. When you reach out to customers and ask them to talk back, they do, in droves, and they relish the opportunity.

This is an emotional outcome that many in marketing miss. Those of us who sell things often view our marketing efforts as pitches — ways to convince the customer to open up his or her wallet and buy right now. And that's not entirely wrong. But to truly cement a relationship and create a lifelong customer, a marketing message must do more than sell. It must converse. It must open a dialogue. And you must be ready to respond. Customers will talk back to you whether they see you on a bus panel or receive an e-mail asking for their best greeting card lines. The question then becomes: Are you ready to embrace the dialogue?

Research Conversations

Of all the conversations I have in my daily life, research conversations are the most relevant to my work as CEO. These are the conversations I have not to sell something but to learn something. I have them all the time, and they are often at the root of our most significant successes. These conversations often take place behind the scenes, out of the spotlight, and are certainly not as visible as a bus campaign or a Valentine's Day sweepstakes. But they are conversations that shape my thinking and guide my decision-making.

Here's a good example: I once had a conversation with the summer interns at the investment bank Allen & Company. As part of their internship, the company sets up a series of brown-bag lunches and brings in speakers to talk to them about business, building a career, and life in New York in general. I took this opportunity not just to speak but also to converse.

Sitting around that conference room table, I realized, was a selection of representatives from Generation Tech. This was the next generation of customers, the ones who had grown up digital and would take that technological savvy into everything they did with their lives — their careers, their personal lives, and certainly their buying habits.

I talked to them about my career and about my life as a businessperson in New York — and then I opened the dialogue: Tell me about the social media you use. What do you like about it? Which platforms do you like best? Why are they your favorites?

The conversation was enlightening. Twitter, I found, played little role in their lives. They saw it as a tool used mostly by their seniors and one that did not factor into their own social networking efforts. Facebook, on the other hand, was as indispensable as oxygen. They looked to Facebook to stay in touch with friends and colleagues, to plan social events, and even to stay current on the latest news. It was a communications lifeline. Businesses that did business with Facebook, they told me, were businesses they assumed would be interested in them as customers. The interns were happy to share their views with me, and the lunch quickly morphed from a favor I did for my friends at Allen & Company to a focus group offering up valuable insights into my next generation of customers.

That happens to me all the time. Everywhere I go, I see a potential focus group. When I engaged this group of young strivers, the benefit to me and to my business was immeasurable. I was invited to share my insights with them, but I turned it into a conversation so that the insights flowed both ways. It was a great meeting for all of us.

That lunch is just one example of what I do all the time — and what 1-800-Flowers.com does on a more structured basis. We are always looking for ways to learn about what's going on in the world and how we can move our business forward.

My brother Chris runs a collection of online panels — essentially a series of virtual focus groups. He communicates with these panels on a regular basis. Some are made up of customers. Others are populated by experts in technology. We keep an ongoing roster of them, and there is always room to mix and match and add to them as our research needs change. These are our sounding boards. We ask the participants in these groups questions, listen to their answers, and field their criticisms, all in an effort to inform our business process. These ongoing conversations help us stay close to issues as they develop.

We also conduct traditional focus groups — the kind that take place in a sealed room with a two-way mirror. But no one is happy when I attend one of those. I am not very patient behind the glass. I find sitting behind the mirror unbearable. I watch the conversation and find myself dying to get in on it. I want to join the discussion at the table. I want to ask follow-up questions and, even when the individual running the focus group for us is highly skilled and experienced, I can't help but second-guess the process.

"Oh, why didn't she follow up on that comment? Wait, I want to know more about that topic. Go back!" Watching it happen without being a part of it is torture — for me and for the poor souls trying to run the focus group through my interruptions. These traditional groups are important to any business, to be sure. But I leave them to the experts. I can't watch a conversation without wanting to be involved.

Because I so value research conversations, I run them all the time, wherever I go. I was sitting on a bus once, on the way to an event, and when we were stuck in traffic I started a conversation with my fellow riders: What was the first concert you ever attended? Answers ranged from the Beach Boys to Def Leppard. But I was doing more than passing the time while we waited for the road to clear. As is often true of my process, I was starting a conversation to learn. Who was around me? What were their experiences? What could they teach me and share with me that would inspire my future actions?

I do this wherever I am — at a dinner party, in an airport lounge. I'm always open to find out more about the person across from me. And I find most everyone is happy to share his or her thoughts and feelings. People like to be asked their opinions. Remember, as I said at the beginning of this chapter, everyone's a customer. To that end, everyone I converse with is a focus group subject. Anything that is said informs me. I never miss the opportunity to experience a good conversation.

Conversations with Me

It's not hard to have a conversation with me, if you've got a mind to do that. I make myself pretty accessible. I talk to the people who talk to me — so much so that if I'm tired and I'm traveling via a commercial airline, I try to get a window seat so I'm not tempted to chat with everyone who walks by. And I'm also accessible in the virtual world. My e-mail address is posted online. And I read that e-mail. Often, I respond to it and engage the sender in a miniconversation.

Here's an example: I was sitting at Citi Field watching the Mets one summer evening when I checked my e-mail to discover a lengthy rant from someone I didn't know. "Matt" had seen my brother Chris and me on a rerun of the reality television show *Undercover Boss*. The show had aired for the first time many months before this exchange, but Matt didn't care about that. He had something to say.

Matt didn't have an issue with the show. He had an issue with me. Matt didn't think the financial arrangement we had with the 1-800-Flowers.com franchisee featured on the show was fair. He wanted to tell me — at length — just how unfair it was.

Matt and I had a fundamental disagreement. We were looking at the same arrangement; I thought it was fair and he thought it wasn't. What was I to do about this?

I could have ignored it. Matt hadn't actually asked for a response. He just wanted to have his say, and he had. But I never step away from an invitation to dialogue. I read through his rant, thought about it, and while sitting in the stands and watching the Mets blow yet another lead, I sent him a response.

I acknowledged that we disagreed, and I added that I appreciated the time he'd taken to think through his message to me. Did I convince him? Probably not. But I did not let the image he had of me — of this remote, detached, unconnected business mogul — stand. I turned a rant into a dialogue, and by doing that, I took some of the fire out of his thinking. This is an impact of conversation that many people miss. Sometimes, you don't have to say anything specific to the other party to get a desired result. Sometimes, the fact that you've shown you've heard them, and then responded, is enough to move the other person out of the "hot zone" and into a more rational place.

I knew that I would not be able to convince him that our treatment of the franchisee was fair. He had already made up his mind based on a ten-minute segment of a TV show. However, now that I had gained some credibility with him simply by engaging directly and giving him direct access to me so that he could share his opinion, I knew that the best way to conclude our conversation was to orchestrate a new conversation — one between Matt and our franchisee. In this way, I could show Matt that his opinion was important to me and our company while simultaneously deepening my relationship with the franchisee. Not surprisingly, Matt and the franchisee had a great conversation and both were thrilled that we actually valued their opinions and relationships enough to connect them. To me, that is what real engagement is all about.

Here's another example of that effect of conversation. My customer service team had a customer who was angry and "would only talk to the CEO!" So I called him back. To say he was surprised was an understatement. I'm sure when he demanded to speak to me he didn't really think he was going to get that opportunity. But here I was on the phone with him. I asked him to tell me about his issue. I did not get emotional with him. I listened and told him we would do our best to resolve his issue to his satisfaction. Whether or not our solution satisfied him is hard to say. But he did get one thing he demanded: a conversation with me.

I can't do that all the time — if I did I'd never get any work done, and besides, we have highly trained, fully qualified individuals who handle these conversations professionally for us every day. But once in a while, it makes sense for me to have these individual conversations with customers — via e-mail, via telephone, or when they approach me on an airplane and tell me they've seen my face at the bus stop. You never know when a conversation will lead to an insight. So I never miss the opportunity to engage with others and find out.

The Future of Customer Conversation

We live in an age in which the very nature of conversation is changing. How we converse with customers going forward will be affected greatly by changes in technology and how that technology shapes our cultural expectations. What will the future of customer conversation be like?

Faster

The rise of the digital experience has made everything faster and has therefore altered our expectations of how long anything should take. In the old days, if it took you a week to research a topic, that was reasonable. Today, if it takes a search engine more than five seconds to load a page and give you your answer, you're annoyed and wondering what's taking so long.

This speed effect is also visible in conversation. When we e-mail, we expect a quick response. When we text, we expect an even faster one. All this speedy conversation has a huge impact on business. When your customer e-mails you, he or she watches the clock from the moment the send button is pressed. The time you take to respond, to engage, and to manage this dialogue must be far shorter than it may have been in the pre-digital age. Understand that technology has sped everything to a new level of normal — and that includes your response time when engaging in customer conversations. The customer is faster. Are you?

Smarter

Again, looking at the technology impact, customer conversations will continue to get smarter. The customer expects that you already know his or her basic details and to be able to move right to the meat of the conversation. I saw this in the interns at Allen & Company. When they interact with a merchant online, they expect — they demand — that the merchant already know their preferences and basic information, and be ready to make smart recommendations to them as individuals. There is no way they would tolerate a merchant who failed to use data intelligently to produce targeted marketing messages. One intern made a purchase online and was chagrined to receive a subsequent marketing pitch from that site for a totally inappropriate product. That conversation was over as far as that intern was concerned.

Curated

This is a popular idea in digital circles, which adds a new layer of responsibility for those of us who would like to converse with our customers. Now not only must we offer conversation channels that suit our customers — e-mail, text, phone, social media — we must also be ready to provide interesting interactions and dialogues that intrigue and entice them. This is the art of the curated conversation. It can be digital — a virtual space in which customers are invited to connect with like-minded individuals to exchange information. Or it can be as old-school and real-world as a dinner party. We, as businesses, are in a position to create these conversation opportunities for our customers to enjoy. More and more, they will look to us to step up to this new job.

Customers are everywhere — not just for flower retailers but for every business. And customers are increasingly interested in conversing with the major players in their lives. I cringe when I see companies putting up roadblocks to conversations — phone trees that make it impossible to get a real person, or e-mail addresses that route to nowhere. This flies in the face of what customers want and misses — completely — the opportunity that conversation offers. When our customers talk to us, they give us information. When we talk back, we show them our appreciation and our desire to learn what it is they want so we can serve them better. That's a message you can't plaster on the side of a bus. It comes through only in the dialogue.

LEADERS IN CONVERSATION: ONE CUSTOMER WRITES . . .

Before the age of e-mail, a customer took it upon herself to write me a letter. In it, she expressed her frustration with finding the right centerpiece for her sister's wedding. She wrote: "If anybody can come up with a decent idea, it's you guys."

I took her invitation to converse with her, and I ran with it. I called her to discuss the problem she faced. I asked individuals at my company to work on it and get back to me with their ideas. I kept the idea in my head as I traveled, once stopping in a store to pick up an oversized martini glass. I had an inkling that it might serve in some way, so I brought it back to the office with me.

Eventually, we developed a winning product: our Happy Hour Collection, centerpieces in cocktail form. It began with the Apple Martini Bouquet. We've since added a margarita version. Our customer was right: we were capable of coming up with a decent idea. By engaging us in conversation, she challenged us to do something innovative.

Look at customer communications as an opportunity to converse — not just exchange data or close a sale.

AFTER WORDS: YOU'RE NEVER DONE BRANDING

The work of creating and managing a brand is never really done. This became clear to me soon after I'd made what I thought — at the time — was the definitive move in my career as a brand marketer. I had secured the rights to use the name 800-Flowers. I was sure I'd hit the home run: a company name with the phone number right in it. Genius. I was on my way.

Sitting on a plane to Dallas, I conversed with my seatmate — a Texan with boots, an oversized belt buckle, and a substantial hat above us in the overhead compartment. He was in oil. (Or "earl," as he said several times until I managed to understand him.) I told him I was in the flower business, and I told him the name, proudly: "800-Flowers."

"Well, that's nice," he said. "Why didn't you call it 799 flowers?"

And I realized I was not as done with my brand as I'd thought. It was a bit of cold water on my big moment. But also an important lesson and one I share often with colleagues. Branding is ongoing work.

NEXT STEPS: MAKE SPACE

If you want conversations to happen regularly, it helps to create a space that encourages them. I set out cheap plastic chairs in my first flower store—not because they looked good but because they encouraged people to sit down and spend some time talking to us. When I set up headquarters for my company, I made sure the layout included not just places to work, but places to chat. Chairs, sofas, gathering spaces. People will converse over cubicle walls or around a water cooler if they must. But if you want to encourage the chatter, make sure the furniture suits the conversational style.

McCANN'S PRINCIPLE NUMBER THREE: CONVERSE FOR INTIMACY, NOT EFFICIENCY

If you're watching the clock, you're not conversing. This is true whether you're interviewing a job candidate or manning a customer service terminal. Speed encourages an efficient exchange of information, but unhurried conversation bonds individuals and reveals truths.

4

—

Conversations with Family

F AMILY IS IMPORTANT. Few would argue with that. But in today's busy world we find an ongoing debate over the role of family in business life. It seems today that you see a lot of anxiety over the issue of work-family balance. Many say technology makes it harder for a committed worker to separate and have family time. The work-family debate seems to center on how to keep the two far apart.

I believe the separation may be part of the problem. From my earliest years on, family has played an integral role in my work life. The two are intertwined. My work and my family experiences inform one another. I learn from all of those who surround me, whether they are my relatives or my colleagues or, in some cases, both. But while my situation may be a bit unusual since mine is a family business, I do think the connection between work and family is genuine. The path to success in both spheres is not to separate but to embrace and connect them. The more that work and family meld in your life, the less tension there will be to deal with, and you will be more connected and contented in both arenas.

In this chapter, I'll look closely at the family conversations that have been important to me in my work life. Over the years, I've come to understand that work and family don't need to be separated or balanced, but integrated as part of a broader human experience. They exist in all of us, all the time.

Conversations with My Elders

Growing up in Queens, I don't remember anyone talking about work-family balance. It was a concept that had not yet made its way into the local discourse. Instead, we had work-family conversations all the time, every day. Work and family made up the primary building blocks of life in my neighborhood, and rather than separate or balance them, we simply lived them. I think back on that time often and recall it as an important and formative experience. I learned early that work and family went hand in hand.

Some of my earliest and more important conversations about work came when I talked with my grandmother. Margaret Mc-Cann was a strong, outspoken lady who ran what would today be considered a thriving management consulting business from her kitchen table. There, family and sometimes friends would gather to talk about the workday.

Sometimes the conversation would be about the day-to-day operation of my father's painting business. As I've told the story many times over the years, on Sundays, we would go over to Grandma's for dinner. My father would get there early and work up job estimates, dictating them to Grandma. The next morning, the estimates would be all ready for him. She was an important and hands-on participant in the workings of the business. Sometimes, the table would fill with friends and family, there would be drinks all around, and the ideas would flow — ideas for new business ventures, ideas for new relationships or partners. The word "brainstorm" had not yet emerged into our local lexicon, but that's what happened around that table all the time.

I was profoundly influenced by these conversations — this casual and constant back-and-forth that flowed within the family setting. It was a constant hum of conversation that shaped the businessman I would be come. Sometimes Grandma would direct her comments to me in a more targeted way. I remember one discussion about the split personality some successful businessmen seemed to project: "He's an animal in business, but after work on the golf course, he's a real gent." My grandmother didn't buy that line.

"Baloney, Jimmy," she used to say. "You are what you are and you don't change who you are just because it's business!"

Was that good business advice? Maybe, maybe not. An MBA might advise a businessperson to adopt a business persona. But my conversations with my grandmother were not just about business advice — they were bound up with life advice. She was the embodiment of the work-family combination that was so much a part of my upbringing. When she advised me to pay my debts rather than seek to shed them, she wasn't talking to me about just business. She was talking to me about life and the kind of life I should build for myself. Work and family were never separate for Margaret McCann, and everything she told me was bound up in those two connected elements. She didn't want me to be just a good businessman. She wanted me to be a good man — in everything I did. There were no separations in her mind, and she didn't want or expect me to divide the two either.

Ultimately I took Grandma's advice. I remained the same man in my personal and professional lives. I am not one man in the boardroom and another on the golf course. The values I hold when I deal with friends and family are the values I bring to my business.

Grandma was a powerful voice in my early days in business. No less so was my father — although he didn't always transmit his wisdom via traditional conversation. He was not the type to sit down and share emotions with you. It just wasn't his way. Much of what I learned from him, I learned by watching.

It was my father who taught me to network. He was a networking pro long before the term was in vogue. He spoke all the time to me about the value of relationships in marketing — if the monsignor at St. Agnes likes your jokes and thinks you did a good job painting the rectory kitchen, he'll tell Father Meara at Trinity, whose brother John owns two apartment buildings. The business follows the relationship. My father was good at this and never lost an opportunity to tell me about it.

I've often shared my memories of the times he used to take me with him to the annual convention of the Painting and Decorating Contractors of America in the Catskills each summer. I watched him work the room, make connections, and build his business through conversations across tables of cold borscht, hot blintzes, and potato knishes. New friends, new customers, new ideas. This was a lesson I took forward into my business career.

I'm a frequent attendee at gatherings of business thinkers. For many years, Marylou and I have had the privilege of attending Allen & Company's Sun Valley Conference. It's an inspiring collection of business minds coming together for the purpose of connecting, conversing, and seeing where that conversation takes us. The Catskills are a long way from Sun Valley — a place where borscht and blintzes are rarely on the menu — and yet I still employ the conversation skills I learned watching my father work a roomful of painting contractors. Handshakes, conversations, relationships, everyone propelled forward into new and better experiences.

Some of my father's advice was more direct. I learned a good lesson from him as a young man when I worked in his contracting business. One day, while on the job with my dad, he chewed out two workmen for being sloppy. After he left, the two guys started venting, cursing my father. I jumped to my father's defense and the three of us tangled. It wasn't a good outcome. Not only did I get roughed up, when I told my father what had happened, he wasn't happy.

"You're the boss's son," he told me. "Of course they're going to curse me out. You have to ignore it." He then set about the unpleasant task of replacing the two workers.

That was a very short conversation that stayed with me a long time. It taught me an important skill — selective hearing. In this digital age, that skill has never been more important. The world is full of chatter, and not all of it is charitable. When you go into business, you can expect that not everyone will love you. When you put your name and your face out in the forefront, you can assume that you'll get some negativity tossed back your way. My father's advice has served me well. *Ignore it.* You can't leap into every nasty exchange and do battle. You'll end up as I did that day on the painting job — bedraggled, angry, and having convinced no one of your superior moral position. Ignore the nastiness. Hear what you have to hear and let the rest go. You'll be happier and more productive.

But perhaps the most important lessons I learned from my father revolved around the conversations he didn't have — or the ones he waited too long to begin. These were conversations with my uncles. As in many family businesses, there was tension in my father's work life with his relatives. Over the years, the tension built and the negative feelings began to overwhelm the relationships. As I look back on them, these were missed opportunities for conversation — a sharing of feelings and hopes and dreams that should have happened but didn't. Why not? Perhaps personal or cultural or generational issues held my father and my uncles back from attempting this sort of discussion.

What I saw was the fallout. One uncle even broke from the family altogether and didn't speak to his relatives for years. Since my father's death, there has been some reconciliation among the family members, but it's a rift that did damage and a situation that I believe could have been avoided. Squabbles over money are not uncommon. There is never enough money to make everyone happy, and that was certainly true of our high-effort, low-margin business in middle-class Queens. But my experience in business has made me realize how critical a conversation can be when this sort of tension flares. Certainly, bottling it up and never addressing it goes to no good end.

Conversations with My Peers

The conversations of my youth helped to shape and guide me in those early years. But I find that the words that flow among my family continue to impact me today. I turn all the time to those of my own generation in the family to talk about what is happening to us, where we have been, and where we are going.

Certainly, this is heightened by the fact that we are a family business and so many of us work together on a daily basis. My brother Chris is the company's operational leader, in charge of the company's day-to-day efforts. We talk all the time — about things that are happening in the company, business decisions that have to be made, everyday shop talk. But we also talk in a way that only brothers can — a kind of shorthand only we understand.

Here's one example and it's a story I've told many times. Chris and I have ten years separating us, so we were never the classic sibling rivals. He was fourteen when I was already a business owner. It was at that time he started to work for me at Flora Plenty — one of my early retail incarnations. At the time, we used a storage space that shared a cellar with a busy Chinese restaurant. One night when the cellar flooded, we were down there to salvage our flowers from the soupy mess. Chris lost his balance and fell into the — well, I'm not even sure what to call it. He smelled so bad when he came out that I made him sit on a drop cloth in the back of the car. When we got home that night, I hosed him off in the backyard and threw his clothes in the trash.

That's a night we both remember when we think about how far we've come in the world. It's also a touch point — a reminder to us both that we came from modest beginnings and that whatever success we have achieved we are still the McCann brothers from Queens. Between us, the conversation might go:

"Feel like some Chinese food?"

And that's all it takes for us to recall the night in the cellar, awash with floating fish heads and soy sauce and restaurant debris. Some conversations are short and bring you back to reality in a hurry.

In case you haven't noticed, I have a tendency to mix work and family. Holidays when most families take the day off tend to be some of the busiest workdays in our industry — we're all scrambling to make sure the centerpieces get to your table, to be sure your mom gets her bouquet. No holidays for us! So when my family gathers (late) on Christmas or (a few days after) Mother's Day, someone will say, "Oh, let's not talk shop." But eventually we will. I'm in the business, and so are my brother, my sister, and other relatives. There just isn't a wall we raise between our business and family lives.

That said, some of the most important conversations I've had have been far from my business life. They are the conversations I have with my wife, Marylou.

Here's one. We had a great Christmas recently at my home on Long Island. It was busy and boisterous with dozens of guests. Family came from all over; we had a grab bag for the adults and gifts for the kids. Once everyone had left, the place was littered with wrapping paper and others signs of a great party. I loved it, but afterward I felt blue. I couldn't shake it. I thought about how quickly the kids had grown, how they now had spouses and kids of their own. How busy their lives were and how full of their own work and family demands they had become. With all that going on, I wondered, how much longer would I be able to host these gatherings? How many more years would the kids want to trek out to my place for the day? How soon before their own lives took them in different directions, perhaps away from the business, away from our base in New York? Would we be able to do this same gathering next year?

That sparked a conversation with Marylou — one I've had with her more than once. She said what she always says: "Live in the moment. Don't worry about what might happen next year. Think about what is happening right now. We had a wonderful day, a wonderful holiday."

She reminds me — over and over — that change will come on its own and although it may be my job to worry about the future, to enjoy life I must also live in the present.

Some conversations are ways to reset a connection. They do not reveal anything new. Rather, they reveal what has always been present but that perhaps you've lost sight of for the moment. My conversations with my family members often do that. They remind me where I've been and where I am, and what's important.

Conversations with My Children

I am asked all the time about how to manage difficult conversations. How do you fire someone? How do you handle a disagreement with a vendor? What's the best way to soothe an angry customer? All these conversations are hard, but they are not the most difficult conversations to have. If you really want to have a tough conversation, talk to your children.

Children offer us the steepest conversation challenges we will ever face. We have so much we want to tell them. They are so often so intent on rejecting everything that comes to them from a place of parental authority. On a comparative basis, firing is easy; talking to an adolescent is hard.

How to do it? Here's what I've learned:

Pick your location

Kids will be more likely to hear you if you're not competing with the other noise in their lives. One of the most significant conversations I've had with my middle son took place in the car as we drove out to visit my brother Kevin, who is developmentally disabled and lives in a group home. I had a lesson I wanted to teach my son — about networking and relationships and how valuable they are in life and in business — but I was having trouble getting my point across. My other two children had readily embraced the network they'd been born into, the one I'd built through my business. They had no second thoughts about plugging into that network and making it their own.

My middle child had a different reaction to his place in that network. He wanted to succeed "on his own," and not through my connections. This was an argument we'd had many times. I wanted to have this conversation with him, but I didn't want to argue. So I picked my location for the conversation: the car.

Without the space of a whole house around us, without the distraction of the TV or his siblings or any other stimuli, we were able to have this exchange. I talked to him about what I'd learned — that success was really about access and finding a way to get people to see you. It's not wrong to trade on a contact or a relationship. It's the way business works — and it works best when it's not a one-way street. I told him a story about how I've done a favor for the son of a vendor and how that wasn't just me being nice, but also a way for me to cement that relationship. As a result, we have each helped the other many times over the years.

I had a lot of examples to share about how relationships are not "cheating" but rather the building blocks to success for both parties. The car setting helped me get through my list without my teenager wandering off. The experience reminds me that any tough conversation requires a smart choice of location, no matter whom you're talking to.

Get help

Sometimes you can't handle a tough conversation alone. Even the most skilled speaker needs a partner once in a while to really bring the point home. My family — specifically my daughter — taught me this lesson.

One year I thought it would be a great idea to take the family on vacation to Disney World. Somehow my teenage daughter didn't see it that way. I was sure that if I just talked to her about it, though, she'd see the light. I recall pulling out all my best persuasive tactics to bring her around, telling her how much fun this was going to be. I was getting nowhere fast: the more I talked, the more my daughter responded with her flat-out rejection of what I was sure was the best vacation idea ever.

Fortunately for all of us, my wife could see the problem. She stepped in to take over the conversation. Rather than having me stand there and continue to make my points, she went to our daughter and started the conversation over. This time, my daughter went first, spilling all her concerns about how a family trip might interfere with her carefully constructed social life, expressing her views as to how she thought the summer should go. In the end, Marylou was successful in getting my daughter onboard with the family vacation plan — something I and my finely honed conversation skills had been unable to accomplish. Sometimes, even the best talker needs a partner.

This is a lesson that follows me in my work on a regular basis. My work with Chris is very much a partnership. We are often referred to as "the two at the top," a management term coined by Peter Ueberroth, a famous entrepreneur. Our management style allows us to execute the tag-team tactic that Marylou employed with our daughter. When one voice is not getting through, a second can break the impasse and bring the conversation to an agreeable outcome. Chris and I will often play this role for each other — providing the second voice when needed in a tough conversation.

Be prepared for their lead

I love to tell the story of the time I took my son on a business trip with me, and on the plane ride home he turned to me and asked, "Dad, do you love what you do?"

I told him that I did. He responded by sharing what he'd heard from his friends: fathers who couldn't wait till the end of the week to get away from the office. My son had never seen me act like that. He even said he could never really tell when I was on vacation. "It's usually involved with business and the whole family goes. It all seems to be part of the same thing."

In that moment, my son had taken us both into one of the unscheduled and memorable moments of our relationship. You can't put the kids on the calendar and schedule moments when they will reveal to you their hopes and dreams. You also can't schedule when you'll be able to convey to them your wisdom and advice. You have to be ready when the moment happens.

The Role of Family in Business

How much of a role should family play in today's business world? This is a debate that has been going on around my conference tables for years. Years ago, we had a high-level ad agency come in to advise us on our marketing and public relations practices. These guys thought our old family business image was antiquated. It had to go. Don't talk so much about being a family business, they said. That shouldn't be your image in the world. It's old-fashioned, not edgy and modern. Instead, they told us, avoid mentioning the fact that you're a family business and focus instead on your technology. You want to change your image from family business to technology pioneer.

We thought about that. Was it time to ditch our image as a family business?

In the end, we decided to ditch the agency instead. Family is not just our image; it's the nature of who we are and how we operate. And it's not just my family that courses through the veins of this company. All of us come to work with the goals and dreams of our families as part of our mental landscape. You can't just leave a part of your life that big in the car when you come into the building. It just doesn't make sense that anyone can.

One thing I've learned is that family is part of what makes for a great business relationship. When you want to impress me and make me your customer or your vendor or your employee for life, don't do something for me. Do something for my family. That I'll remember forever. I saw that happen at a gathering of 1-800-Flowers.com franchisees. At the event, we had with us a senior staffer who had served recently in the military. After one of the presentations, a franchisee approached the staffer with a question — not related to the flowers business but related to the military. The franchisee's son had been recently assigned to a new and dangerous mission. He wanted to know if the staffer had any advice for the young soldier.

The staffer responded immediately. Have your son call me tonight, he said. And the call happened — the veteran spent time on the phone with the young soldier, talking to him about his assignment, his options, his path to success, and what might lie ahead for him. I heard about this phone conversation the next day when the franchisee found me at a cocktail reception and told me all about it. As I watched our Flowerama franchisee Ken Rogers speak, I understood the value of mixing business with family and how both areas of your life can work together for the ultimate good. There was no obvious business reason for my staffer to reach out to this young solider. But he did it, and as a result this franchisee felt a stronger bond to us as business partners. Mixing work and family combines the two things in life that many people value most. When these elements work together, they drive success all around.

The effect of this travels beyond individual relationships and informs the larger relationship between customer and retailer. I came across a great promotion recently from a winery that ran a sweepstakes, and as a prize, instead of money, wine, or a celebrity appearance, it offered an all-expenses-paid family reunion. That reveals a clear understanding of how family plays a role in every aspect of life. What we really want in life is a happy family — we want our work to help us have a happy family, we want the retailers with which we do business to help us have a happy family. We don't keep our families separate. We think about them all the time. We seek out individuals and businesses who support us while we do that.

When you want to have an impact on me, don't do something for me. Do something for my family. That I will never forget. That's true if you're my employer, my vendor, my business associate, or the retail store in my neighborhood.

LEADERS IN CONVERSATION: THE OUTSIDER'S VIEW

Sometimes it takes someone outside the family to remind you how important family is.

I had lunch with Wayne Huizenga, another friend and business hero of mine, who built Blockbuster Video, Waste Management, Inc., and AutoNation, among other companies. He helped me see this reality.

I traveled with Chris one day to Wayne's home in Florida. We had a four-hour lunch, and during this conversation I sought Wayne's advice. My company, I felt, was at a crossroads and I had to make decisions about how to move forward and spur growth.

Wayne made an important observation. He talked that day about a decision I had made recently to make all our stores company-owned. This move, he said, while perhaps financially sound, was moving away from a core element of the company's being. It was undermining the theme of the family-owned business.

When a company owns stores, it becomes a corporate entity. When franchisees operate stores, they do it on a family-by-family basis. Franchising keeps you closer to your family business roots, he said. It allows you to grow while never moving too far away from who 1-800-Flowers.com really is—a family operation.

That conversation was one that helped me see my company in a new way and understand the values—family values—that had always been part of our success.

AFTER WORDS: MIXING FAMILY AND BUSINESS

I once had a conversation with a partner about why we shouldn't be partners anymore.

"You're not happy and I'm not happy," he said. "We both need to find a way to move forward and I think it may mean that we don't move forward together."

I realized later that my business partner and I had engaged in an important kind of conversation that day—one that opened the situation we were both in to an entirely different resolution than the one we had planned. Each of us went into the conversation willing to make it a moment of change, rather than a discussion of the status quo. It was a generous conversation in which we released each other and gave each other the permission to move forward. It was a purely business conversation, but it is one that I was able to recount later to my father, and we were able to use it to diffuse a long-standing family dispute. I suggested to my father—as it had been suggested to me that day by my business partner—that perhaps his dispute needed to be reexamined, with entirely new goals set for the individuals involved. These were two conversations in very different places—different goals, different players. But a common theme joined them. When I could see the crossover, I was able to learn from one and be more successful in the other.

NEXT STEPS: SAY THE WRONG THING

Sometimes, in order to get to the right answer, you have to be willing to say the wrong thing. It had been taboo for years to talk about the tension that had built up between my father and my uncles over the family business. When I was able to insert that unmentionable topic into conversation, we were able to resolve an issue that had resulted in years of discord. Too often, we are silent for fear of saying the wrong thing. But it takes courage to step into the difficult conversation and try.

McCANN'S PRINCIPLE NUMBER FOUR: CONVERSE AS THOUGH YOU ARE SITTING AT YOUR KITCHEN TABLE

The most memorable conversations are the ones we have with family. Use what you learn at home—such as how to honor traditions, manage conflict, and hear both good and bad news—to make your business conversations meaningful.

5

Conversations about Technology

OR THOSE OF YOU surfing the Internet, trying to find the
next great technology innovation, stop it. Stop clicking. Stop
staring at your screen in the hopes it will reveal the answers.
The best way to tap into the latest in technology is through conversation: interaction with the brightest and most innovative technology players across business disciplines.

In this chapter, I'll relate how I learned to stay abreast of technology by looking up from my screen and across a dinner table.
I'm not only referring to the top technologists I have access to now
as a CEO. I've been practicing this art for years — long before I
had enough status to count on that kind of access. The real key is
to show your genuine interest. Most people — your IT guy, your
game-addicted friend, your children (or grandchildren) — would
be happy to tell you about their new gadgets or other innovations
at work in their lives. Take the opportunity to engage in conver-

sations about technology. The results, I have found, can be both interesting and profitable.

I have always been fascinated by new technology. I am an eager early adopter, and I never tire of talking about what the digital age will bring us next. Information technology is the force of our times — our Industrial Revolution — and we are still in its earliest years. With so much to come, we would be remiss to not start the conversation now.

Why Embrace Technology?

Technology is a profitable tool for business — no question about that. But that's not the only reason I study its development so closely. Technology is a fundamental connection point for humanity. It is a force that brings us all closer together.

Our relationship with technology has been fraught in recent years. Many say technology has had a negative effect on conversation. They say that technology is a wall that blocks us from one another, keeping us apart and isolating us in digital enclaves. They rail against technology as the prime foe of real human connection.

It's simply not so. Even as we bring technology into our lives, we do so as a result of our underlying human desire to connect. We use technology not to drive other human beings away but to be more connected to them — more quickly, more intensely — than we ever could have been before. Technology is a force for connection. Innovations in digital media facilitate the relationships we have and give us more opportunities to share and be present in each other's lives. The potential for the digital space to be a place of conversation is enormous and is emerging now in our forums, our blogs, and our social networks. The Internet hums with global conversations. Business can foster this presence by creating platforms and opportunities for connection and conversation.

Our Technological History

Our company has always been on the cutting edge of new technology — no matter where it emerged. It may not seem very technologically savvy now, but we were considered pretty aggressive back in the day, when we made our name and our 800 number one and the same. The 800 number (back then) was considered a creative and edgy way to do business. It sounds almost retro now, but at the time we were really pushing the envelope.

But that was just the beginning. Throughout the history of my company, I have looked for ways for us to embrace new technology and lead business forward into new territory.

We were the first retailer to strike marketing deals with CompuServe and AOL. At the time, AOL was the main portal for new users of the Internet. We were there when they came online for the first time — the first e-tailer in their lives as e-shoppers.

We have been early to the new digital opportunities of the modern era — striking one of the first deals with Facebook, leveraging social media to connect with customers, and coming up with new technological ways for our customers to connect with each other. Consider, for example, Celebrations.com, a site we launched for customers to come together and get information, share ideas, and be part of conversations around celebrations. Celebrations .com is our entry into social commerce — a subset of e-commerce that involves using social media, online media, social interaction, and user contributions to assist in the online buying and selling of products and services.

Going forward, we are constantly looking for new ways to improve the customer experience, to connect with our customers and help our customers connect with each another. What I've learned in my years at this job is that great technology does not spring fully formed from an R&D lab. It does not arrive ready to plug and play. Instead, it starts with people.

Talking Tech

Our conversations around technology take place in a variety of situations.

My brother Chris and another member of our management team recently had an extended conference call with Vinton Cerf. Vint is a leading tech innovator who served as VP and Chief Internet Evangelist for Google. Around our office, we all joke that Al Gore took all the credit for Vint's invention. Chris met Vint at an innovation conference years ago, and the conversation between them has been going on ever since.

On that conference call, Vint was giving us feedback on our website. There was an aspect to the way we were handling customer rewards that didn't feel quite right to him — he spent half an hour giving Chris his detailed analysis of what was not working and how to fix it.

At one point, Vint apologized for being so picky. Chris and our executive couldn't tell Vint fast enough what a help he was and how grateful we were that he'd taken the time to tell us what he'd observed.

This is a good story because it illustrates the value of conversation in the technology space. Our access to a mind as talented as Vint Cerf's was born out of conversation — a human connection fostered by Chris the first time the two men met. It continues to serve us as a business and, by extension, our customers, again through conversation — Vint on the phone, talking us through the changes that could be made to the site to help create an optimal experience. Certainly, all this information could be exchanged digitally, without direct human interaction, but I would suggest that if we relied on machines alone to connect with Vint Cerf, we would never have been able to fully benefit from all he knows. The human aspect of the connection is what truly opened his knowledge to us. Think about that the next time you want to "network" by shooting someone an e-mail. If Chris had done that, would the connection have been as deep and as valuable?

Vint is not our only adviser on issues of technology. We have a very impressive board of directors, and there is no shortage of innovative ideas coming from that group. Jim Cannavino is a former senior executive at IBM and has a wealth of knowledge about IT. Jim began work at IBM at the age of eighteen. Over the years, he ran both the mainframe business and, later, the personal computer division. He has been very helpful in providing insight into our architecture and recently provided useful information for the acquisition of a point-of-sale (POS) system from one of our partners.

We also routinely reach outside our own circle for additional input. Chris makes regular trips to technology-related conferences to stay engaged in cutting-edge developments. Chris and a number of our employees recently attended Google Atmosphere,

Google's innovation conference. It was a virtual storm of ideas. Chris has already adopted one: using Google technology to help us track our shipments. Google Atmosphere creates an environment for business leaders to explore new ways of working, through a combination of industry experts discussing emerging business models, customers sharing stories of how they are transforming their business, and experts unveiling new products. These are what you might call curated conversations — they are thoughtfully organized gatherings of individuals who want to connect and discuss the trends and themes of the technology business. An exchange of white papers just wouldn't be the same.

Conversation is so important to our technological process that I look for ways to systemize it and ensure that it continues routinely in our firm. As an example, I've organized a series of dinners where I invite interesting, tech-savvy people — from within and outside our company — to sit around a table, enjoy a good meal, and discuss the latest and greatest in technology and marketing.

These dinners are enormously valuable to me because they keep me surrounded by intelligent conversation about technology. If I call up any one of these individuals and set up a meeting, I know that they will be happy to come by and talk tech with me. But the atmosphere of the dinner party really gets the conversation going. The wine and the conversation flow, ideas put forth and tossed about by people who really know what's going on out there in the digital space. This is more than just your average brainstorming session. It's a setting that allows for a higher level of discussion. Because it's off-hours, away from the office, somehow that allows for a freedom of thought and a passion of delivery that might not happen otherwise.

It is often from these dinners that we as a company are able to take action and fuel new ideas to benefit our customers. For instance, I organized one dinner that was primarily internal — mostly Flowers staffers talking about what we had accomplished in recent months and what we could do in the future to differentiate ourselves from the competition. It was during this dinner that our head of technology talked about an idea he'd been working on — a way to "close the loop" of gift-giving by creating a way for the recipient to say thanks with a single click. This was a more robust version of a delivery confirmation. Certainly, our customer wanted to know if Grandma *got* the flowers, but what our customer really hoped to hear was that Grandma *liked* the flowers. Our head of technology talked for a bit about how he hoped to make that happen — giving the recipient an easy way to send an e-mail, perhaps add a video, and convey the emotional response to the gift.

As I listened, my mind went back to my time on First Avenue in our first flower shop. Those were the days when we ran a street-level shop and customers would stop by sometimes just to have a cup of coffee and chat. They'd share how they felt about all kinds of things, including the flowers they'd received from us. We, in turn, could share with them.

"Bob, nice to see you. Your grandmother was just here in the shop yesterday. She *loved* the flowers."

I realized as I listened to the discussion about this new technology in development that what was being described was a digital manifestation of those old neighborhood conversations. Sometimes, in e-commerce, we send e-mails or other digital data only when we're unhappy — when something needs to be resolved.

What I was hearing that evening at dinner was a way to use the digital connection to re-create that positive interaction—"By the way, I loved the flowers. Thank you!"

Creating that conversational space in a dinner setting helped me to see the value of the new technology and how it could be used to improve the customer experience. Would I have seen the same possibility if my head of technology had delivered his information in a PowerPoint deck in a conference room? Maybe. But it would not have been the "aha!" moment—the visceral connection I had to a time in my own retail life when human conversation was a daily event. The unique context helped clarify it for me.

I'm a true fan of the meal-as-conversation platform. I've made that point many times in many different ways, but I think it's particularly important to use this tactic when talking about technology. We tend to see technology as a tool—a way to make money, be more efficient, be faster and more targeted. And it does all those things. But it is also a manifestation of who we are as human beings—the next generation of our creative efforts—and how our technology makes people feel is vitally important. If the discussion of technology takes place only on-screen, the human response may be lost.

Technology discussions are so important to my company that we keep them going even after most people would have said goodbye. Our head of application development left us recently. Normally this would have been an unpleasant event, but we turned it into a positive one that will yield benefits far into the future. Instead of sending our former employee on his way—maybe with a bit of resentment at his leaving—we decided to finance the new company he was starting. This not only enabled his company to get on its feet much more quickly, it also provided us with continued access to his ideas and experience, something that will continue to pay off long into the future. We took "good-bye" and turned it into an ongoing dialogue that now benefits two firms — and two sets of customers.

Where Technology Is Going

The next evolution of marketing is taking place over social media. This is the technology that the conversation business must master to be successful. At its earliest stages, social media has been a personal rather than a business conversation. It's a space where we gossip, talk about our weekends, and post pictures of our babies, vacations, and home improvement projects. But the speed and passion with which people have adopted social media indicate that business needs to catch on, and quick.

This is an opportunity many businesses are missing. I am often asked by smaller retailers to give advice. Most expect I will tell them something about their physical stores or perhaps suggest a marketing plan. But these days, I advise routinely that the next step for small business is social media — it is the medium in which the customer now wants to engage in conversation. In the old days, on First Avenue, they came in for coffee. Perhaps people don't do that any longer — perhaps they don't have the time or regular customers don't live nearby the way they used to. But that does not mean that your customer doesn't want to share with you what's on her mind. She does. She wants to chat, casually, conveying her interests and her expectations. It doesn't mean she wants to participate in your focus group or respond to your telephone survey.

But she does want you to know that she's got a *huge* Christmas list this year and it's *so hard* to find something that will impress Aunt Sally, and plus, all the family will be coming to her house this year and she wants to make it special. These are the conversations that tell a retailer what he must do next to make a sale. And if they're not stopping by the shop to tell you all this, you must meet them where they are conversing — in the social media space.

Our head of technology was on his honeymoon when we called him and asked him to pack up and come join us in a meeting with executives from Facebook. He wasn't thrilled that we'd interrupted his honeymoon (and I can only imagine what his new wife must have said when he told her), but the opportunity to work with the heavyweight champion of social media was too good to pass up. We found in our work with Facebook that we could not only converse with our customers in this new space, we could also facilitate connections among them.

We started out on Facebook by using our page to provide customer support. But thanks to the insights posted there, we saw we could do more. As part of our work with Facebook, 1-800-Flowers .com added buttons to our e-commerce site, letting visitors "like" a particular bouquet or other product they that would be happy to receive. Every time customers clicked "Like," the action triggered a story in their friends' news feeds — and that flower power meant people were talking to their friends about the brand. We were able to look at the business through a Facebook lens.

This is a story first told as a Facebook Success Story on the Facebook.com site. In the weeks leading up to the holiday we asked moms to "like" the products they most wanted to receive as a gift. After Mother's Day we ran the numbers and found that four out of the five most-liked products turned out to be our Mother's Day bestsellers. The Facebook status updates helped inspire kids to get their moms what they really "liked" for Mother's Day. We felt great. We'd made connections for our customers and generated sales for our bottom line.

Appreciating technology and deploying it successfully in a company can be two different things. Certainly I've met many corporate leaders who admire and use technology personally but still struggle to deploy it successfully in their businesses. I've learned that doing so is a complicated process that requires a combination of effort to keep the conversation going and knowledge of how to move that discussion into action when the time is right.

Make Tech Conversation a Part of Everyday Chatter

Anyone can show up at a meeting with a presentation. To really strike the new ideas that are bubbling up, you often need to tap into the more casual chatter that takes place around the office every day. The informal banter among colleagues can set off the discussion that changes a company.

To make that happen, we don't let our IT guys hide in their own corner of the building. In some companies, IT isn't just its own department, it's its own planet, and few without multiple PhDs dare venture into the technology inner sanctum. At Flowers, we set up the office to keep that from happening. Our head of technology has his office just down the hallway from Chris and me. That means we cross paths all day. These are not meetings, just casual interactions. But they keep us in front of one another, and it's the casual conversations that can make a new idea take off. The interaction between management and technology does not have to be formal. It can be "Hey, what are you working on?" If your tech team works apart from you — down halls, behind closed doors, off in its own little world — a key opportunity to connect is lost.

At the same time, I've found it's equally valid — sometimes — to give technologists their own space to experiment and brainstorm without the pressure of explaining it to all us nontechnical folks right away. This was our experience with the Celebrations concept. I wanted Celebrations to be not just a brand, but also a technological innovation for the business. I wanted us to create a virtual space for customers to converse with one another, to converse with us, and to create and experience community.

When I talked about my idea in the initial meetings around this brand, I called it the "echo chamber" concept. This got me a lot of blank stares. Nobody seemed to really see where I was going with all this. And the technologists I had on the project also seemed unsure how to make this concept work for the brand. So I sent them off to chat among themselves for a while. Literally. We are headquartered in the Long Island town of Carle Place, but I sent the Celebrations team into their own office in New York City. This was their opportunity to engage in "skunkworks" — on their own, apart from the general business chatter of the ongoing 1-800-Flowers.com brand. And in this separate environment, they were able to do what seemed to be so difficult back at the home office. They were able to envision and create this new brand — and the new technology that would make it possible.

This was an important lesson for me and made me adjust my thinking as a conversation strategist. Because it's clear, looking back, that this group needed to step away and have its own conversation before it could come back and talk to all of us in a meaningful and coherent way. It was a lesson to me that some conversations need to be held without management present. Their own space gave our tech team the intellectual freedom to make the idea work.

Going Forward

People still wrestle with the wisdom of bringing technology into our everyday lives. We still worry whether we've gone too far — whether we've lost some element of our humanity as the technology takes over. To that concern I say: relax. We, as human beings, seem to be able to protect ourselves from complete obsolescence.

A favorite story around our office is of the time my brother Chris met an executive from AOL at a conference — we were still in our partnership with the brand at that time. But as Chris talked to her, he made a startling discovery. The executive said she often ordered flowers from us — but not via the AOL connection. She preferred the telephone. After a long day of staring at the screen, she confessed, it was nice to hear another voice on the line.

That was an important exchange for two reasons. One, it reminded us that no matter how technologically advanced human beings have become, we never completely shake our need to talk to another person. That desire to connect is still there. If we'd offered that AOL executive a discount to shop online, she may still have used the phone. The desire to interact with other human beings is a powerful thing.

Two, this also reminded me to stay in touch with our customers even as we add digital elements to our business — to be sure we are still with them, aligned with them, and fulfilling their wishes in the process. As we've learned the hard way, it's possible to go too far.

Years ago, we had a funny experience with a brand-new telephone technology. It allowed our telephone operators to see who was calling and pick up with a personal greeting even before the customer heard the sound of a phone ringing.

We thought: Wow, this is great! It's so fast! It's so targeted!

Our customers, on the other hand, hated it. They thought it was just plain creepy that we knew who they were before they could even hear the phone ringing. They wanted to hear a ring or two to be sure that the call was going through as expected — they were accustomed to that pause, that moment of hearing the phone ring once or twice before a cheery voice came on to take their order. When we jumped in too quickly, we startled them.

I like to tell this story whenever we are considering a new technology. That new telephone technology was certainly new enough. But it never made it out of the testing phase. New is not always better.

Try It

"I'm not really a tech guy."

"That's for the big companies; I'm just a small business."

It frustrates me when I hear businesspeople talk themselves out of trying new technologies. Often, people will tell me they just don't know how to get started on Twitter or Facebook or whatever the new technology happens to be. There are myriad resources available to businesspeople who want to learn, from adult education courses to online tutorials. College campuses are jam-packed with tech-savvy students willing to help as interns or project consultants — that's a smart and efficient way to tap into their expertise and their familiarity with the digital landscape. Google your neighboring merchants to see if they're on Facebook or the new platform du jour. Then call them up and ask them for some advice — or perhaps a referral to their technology consultant.

And ask those who use the technology what they like about it. Many ordinary users will be happy to tell you.

I watched my granddaughter Abigail recently using her mother's iPhone. I watched how this little girl — nursery school age — easily picked up this piece of technology and manipulated it. She's a baby, and yet this machine — this thing I found so amazing and so special when I first saw it — is as ordinary to her as a crayon. Technology is not special for her generation. It's expected, the way I expect there to be paper and pens and a coffee machine. It is a normal part of her everyday existence — and one that will become only more pronounced as she gets older.

I realized while watching her how ingrained technology will continue to be in our world, in our business, in all aspects of our lives. It doesn't matter if you sell flowers or pharmaceuticals or financial services. The way you interact with your customers will become more and more digital as the technology shows us the way. Whether that worries you or excites you, it's the truth. Some people love new technology. Others are afraid of it. But technology is agnostic to our positions. It presents itself in our lives no matter how we feel about it. When we talk about technology, when we learn and share and connect with one another using it, we advance our businesses and the quality of our lives.

Technology can be scary to those who are new to it. I remember once at a gathering of 1-800-Flowers.com florists that one long-time franchisee stood up and asked me point-blank: What would be the relevance of flowers in the digital world?

"Everybody can communicate using technology so quickly and so effectively and with so many different elements like pictures and music — will there still be a reason to send flowers?" she wanted to know.

My response: Of course. In the digital era, a physical product like flowers takes on even more meaning. In a time when we can e-mail and text and post to communicate, the added meaning of a beautiful, natural product like flowers is that much more powerful.

"Digital doesn't replace us," I said. "It reminds everyone why what we do is so important." Technology, I told her, only reminds everyone how beautiful a real flower can be.

If you're not talking about technology, all the time, across departments, across generations, across water coolers and family dinner tables, you are missing out on the trend of our time. That conversation is happening in your office, among your customers and vendors, and in the marketplace all around you. It's up to you to join in, learn about it, and lead.

LEADERS IN CONVERSATION: WHO ARE YOU?

Recently, I asked new members of my mobile technology team to join me for drinks after work. This is a team made up of many young people; some of them knew me well and others knew me just as "the boss." We sat at the bar, and I engaged in my "sing for your supper" process with the group. I started with a newcomer.

"Tell us about yourself," I said.

He began to recite his résumé.

"No, no," I interrupted. "Not about what you've done. About you. Tell us about you. Where were you born? What did your father do for a living? How did you come to New York?"

This was a work gathering, but I moved to give it a personal touch. I encouraged the participants to share who they really were—to find connections, bring emotions to the surface, and foster a sense of social intimacy in this work group.

When I left the group, they were still at the bar, flipping their napkins over to sketch out the ideas they were discussing.

AFTER WORDS: COMMITTING RESOURCES

When you start a conversation, you have to be willing to back it up; for a CEO, that means committing resources to the ideas that flow out of the debate. When the young members of the tech team came in the morning after the bar meeting, I made sure they had access to a conference room and meeting time to continue their brainstorming. It wasn't much, but it was a sign of my support for their ongoing conversation.

NEXT STEPS: TRY THE NEW THING

Just like everything else in life, conversation has been deeply affected by the digital revolution. To stay on top of the trends, I make it a priority to be an early adopter of technology. Touch the screen yourself. Explore the keyboard. Make the effort to participate in the revolution—not just harness it for profit. I've tried to unmask my passion for gadgetry and why I consider it a guiding principle of my business life in this chapter. Use it. Learn about it. Talk about it. Even if you consider yourself "low-tech," put the mental energy into understanding the change around you. Technology is the new platform for conversation.

McCANN'S PRINCIPLE NUMBER FIVE: CONVERSE ACROSS MEDIUMS

There is no one medium for conversation. It can happen in a wide variety of formats. Do not ignore any place the conversation is happening. Keep your ears attuned to where the conversation will migrate next.

6

Learning from Conversation Leaders

I'S ALL WELL AND GOOD for me to go on about using conversation as a leadership tool. But you might well wonder how you can make that happen. Any good businessperson can learn the art of basic conversation and interaction in a business setting. Just go to any networking session and watch everyone get his or her conversation workout. It's a room full of conversation leadership practitioners at work.

But how do you take it to the next level? How do you move up from being a good conversationalist to being a conversation leader? In this chapter, I'll explain why making that leap is closer to your grasp than you realize. It's not easy or quick, but the answer is accessible. The tutors of great conversation leadership are all around us. The question is whether you are ready to reach out and begin the learning process.

Pay Attention in the Presentation

Presentations are a part of everyday work life, so much so that we tend to become desensitized to them. They wash over us. We rely on them for information, but we hardly look to them for lessons in leadership.

In fact, some of the best lessons on conversation leadership are lurking in those PowerPoint presentations. The trick is to watch the great presenters at work and observe how they are taking the most one-sided communication process in our workplace today and turning it into a thousand individual dialogues.

The average presenter gets up in the front of the auditorium or conference room, fiddles with his laptop, and begins the Power-Point presentation. He moves through his material in a workman-like fashion, making sure to explain each of his slides, dropping in the occasional joke to show what a real human being he is, and watching the clock to ensure he does not go too far over his allot-ted time and get the "hook" from his superiors.

That's a presentation we've all been through. It's a run-of-the-mill experience, nothing special, nothing extraordinary.

Now here's how it might work with a master:

"Good morning and thank you for the opportunity to address you today. Before I get started I wanted to let you all know that at the end of my presentation, there will be a short quiz on the material."

Huh?

All of a sudden, the mood in the room shifts. Anyone who had been settling in for a nice, long PowerPoint nap is sitting up. Eyes that had been wandering onto handheld devices shoot upward to the speaker. Shoulders straighten all over the room. A quiz? A quiz!

Immediately, that speaker has changed the dynamic. No longer is he giving a one-way information dump to a grudgingly receptive audience. He's raised the stakes. You can't just sit there like blobs, he's announced. You're going to be quizzed on the material — your reputation for intelligence will be on the line for all to see.

Now he has engaged his audience in a new way. What had been a one-way experience now has an element of charged energy that runs between speaker and audience. It's not the audible conversation that we might think of between two speakers. But it is a two-way communication between presenter and audience. The flow of energy now goes both ways.

I've seen that tactic employed, and the results are dramatic. The presenter is able to move the entire room from passive to active with that one line. Sometimes, a little murmer of skepticism runs through the crowd after the quiz gauntlet is thrown down. Is he kidding? Can he do that? Is there really a quiz? In my experience of watching this tactic employed, nobody in the audience takes the chance. Everyone flips off his game of Tetris and sends back the "Yes, I'm listening" vibe to the speaker. The dialogue has begun.

Why turn a presentation into a dialogue with the audience? It magnifies the impact of your material. You are no longer presenting from the front of the room, you are leading. And your audience isn't just sitting or even following. They are accepting your invitation to join you in the journey. What you now say has power far beyond the data on slides. You've transformed a run-of-the-mill meeting presentation into a leadership moment.

I speak in front of audiences all the time. Sometimes they are internal audiences of Flowers employees or vendors. Sometimes I speak to outside groups. I've addressed groups in all shapes and sizes and stood before audiences in all manner of venues. These are some of the tips I've acquired over the years that help me turn a presentation into a conversation with each member of the audience.

Pick your targets

This may seem counterintuitive if you're hoping to engage the entire audience, but if you single out individual faces on which to focus, you alter your own delivery in subtle ways. Now, instead of being a single voice shouting out to many, you have established a rapport and an eye-contact connection with one or two human beings in the mass before you. Interestingly, this does not cut out the rest of the audience. If your communication is made more robust and more connected, all who hear it will benefit from that level of engagement. Pick a few people in the audience and talk to them. Use them to gauge how you're doing, if you're landing an emotional response, if your jokes are going over as planned. By using these few as a touch point, you'll be better able to secure connection with the larger group.

Hold still

Somewhere in the dark ages of public speaking advice, someone told speakers to move their heads back and forth to sweep the room with a gaze, back and forth. My experience is that just doesn't work. It's distracting to watch the speaker's head move like that. Pick your eyeballs in the audience and move amid that set group. You aren't watching a tennis match.

Talk to women

This is a trick I uncovered after years of standing before audiences and trying to make connections. No matter how good you are up on the stage, you are at the mercy of your audience's cultural experiences. And men, in our culture, are just not an emotive group. They will guard their emotional reactions closely, and most especially in a business setting. They may be truly moved or inspired by what you're saying and you'll never know it while you're up onstage. Perhaps later, in the meet and greet, a man may approach you and let down his guard and talk about the emotions that were engaged by your talk. But while you're talking, he was a stone. Women in an audience, on the other hand, are far more willing to show how they feel about what you're saying. You'll get smiles or frowns or looks of reproach — all manner of emotional responses. This is not a hurdle for women, even in a business setting. They hear, they feel, they have no difficulty with making that known.

For that reason, I often make an effort when I present to pick a few women in the room with whom to make eye contact. It's a way for me to gauge how I'm doing, and also a way for me to pump up my efforts to make my presentation into a dialogue. This give and take of emotion is, in and of itself, a conversation of sorts. We are exchanging our emotional reactions. This is the dialogue I hope to have with the whole room. I find that when you start with the women in the room, you get that kickoff of emotional exchange. If you try it with the men, you may just get stonewalled.

Present from notes

This is an oldie but a goodie and so I'll repeat it here. Don't read to your audience. Make a list of the points you want to cover and then talk to them. There is just no way to read a prepared text without sounding canned. And if you sound canned, those in the audience will give you a canned response: they will sit quietly until you're done, clap politely, and then move on. No conversation there. Make a list of points you want to make, and those are your notes. When you read from a page (or, worse, from a PowerPoint slide), you set up a wall between yourself and the audience. The signal to the audience is: I've got a set presentation to go through, and if you try to interact with me, you'll throw me off my plan. On the other hand, a speaker who sounds less structured, who is working from notes, is more open to engagement with the audience. That's your potential conversation. The reader is giving a performance; the speaker from notes is open to what the audience might want to contribute.

A great presenter takes a moment of one-sided communication and opens it up. It may result in a boisterous question-and-answer session. It may spark side conversations that take place during the break. Or it may make each and every member of the audience feel as if the speaker is talking directly to them. This energy flow is a conversation opportunity. Great presenters make it work.

Observe the naturals

Anytime someone tells me that he'd like to learn better conversation skills if only he had a tutor, I shrug. I tell that person to turn on the TV. Television is a tremendous tool for conversation leadership training? Why? Because it is one of the great platforms for watching natural conversation leaders at work. When you make a list of some of the most powerful conversation leaders of our era, they are not hidden from view. They are in prime time. Watch and learn.

Learning from Bill Clinton

The former president is widely respected as one of the great communicators of our time. His skills range from wowing a room to commanding a world stage. He is respected as a master of the art of speech and conversation in just about any setting.

He's also considered a "natural"—an individual born with the gift of gab. What can we learn from him? Plenty. He is one of the great role models, not just for the art of conversation leadership, but for the ability to learn the skill over time.

It's easy now to see Bill Clinton in his communicative glory—holding a world audience rapt, for example, as he gave the inspiring speech to the Democratic National Convention introducing President Barack Obama. Who can do it like Bill?

But it wasn't so long ago that even Bill himself couldn't do that. In 1988, then governor Bill Clinton had an opportunity to shine on the national political stage. He was offered the chance to give the nominating speech for Michael Dukakis at the Democratic National Convention. He took the stage, faced his audience of fellow Democrats . . .

And flopped.

What everyone remembers from that day was that Clinton was in desperate need of an editor. After an hour, Clinton delivered the line that earned him the most applause of the evening: "And in conclusion . . ."

Ouch.

Watch that speech and notice how Clinton honed his skills over time. From that day at the convention, Clinton kept right on going. He practiced the art of timing. He worked at the process of understanding and connecting with an audience. He learned not to just talk at them, but to connect with them.

What Clinton now does so well:

Make eye contact

This is harder to see on a big stage, but something almost everyone who has met the former president reports. He is scrupulously careful to make eye contact — and to use that to create a moment of connection and intimacy — with everyone he meets. It can be a moment shaking hands or a time asking a question in a small group setting. Clinton radiates this aura of compete attention to the speaker. When you meet him, people say, you feel as if you are the only person in the room with him.

Me, too!

This is a tactic anyone can try, and Clinton makes full use of it. When in conversation with an individual, listen for ways to communicate connection. What is the person saying that you can relate to and share? It can be anything — "You're from New York? I've visited many times." "You have two boys? I'm also a parent." Clinton will often share stories of his youth that create a connection with the listener. Critics were often stunned to hear him share personal details of his life growing up raised by a single mother or his struggles as a young man with self-esteem issues. But these are the "me, too" moments that create intimacy and allow for a deeper conversation to take place.

Keep learning

Clinton has tremendous natural personal gifts, but he did not stop there. He has spent his life learning his communications craft. This is perhaps the most inspiring aspect of Clinton as a conversation leader. He is always learning. The young up-and-coming politician who went on too long at the Democratic National Convention took his critique to heart, worked on the problem, and came back with stronger skills. He worked what he had, and he always looked for ways to make it better. Any leader can learn from this process. No matter how good you are, you can improve.

Learning from Oprah Winfrey

I admit it — I've had my "Oprah" moments. There are times in my everyday life as a CEO when I need to tap into my inner Oprah to get the job done. She has a lot to teach us all.

One of the primary lessons I've learned from Oprah is that great conversations happen when the boss turns over the mic and lets the rest of the room start talking. Certainly, this is the secret of Oprah's television success. We tune in not to hear Oprah speak, but to hear Oprah get everyone else to speak. This works in a business setting, too.

Routinely, my company throws a party to meet and welcome new hires to the team. I get up and give my usual pep rally speech — and then I hit my Oprah mode. I take the mic and I walk it around the room, handing it to random people and asking them to talk. And they do. They tell us their war stories about making a customer happy, handling a rush job, coming up with a powerful new idea. The room buzzes with energy. And all because I — the Oprah of the event — managed to stop talking long enough to let others take the lead.

When you watch Oprah work — or all great talk show stars — you see their secret: the way they use conversation leadership to achieve their own goals of a great show. They speak, they listen, then they encourage others to talk back. This is delicate since they have the status of being a star, being on television, being the person in control. A CEO has that same status in his or her own company. So the art of being a leader and leading the group to conversation requires practice. Not everyone will feel brave enough to step up and converse with you the first time. You need to do it over and over so that when your employees see you coming at them with the mic, they know what you want and they'll step up and talk back.

Learning from Charlie Rose

Given the "gotcha" nature of today's media, it's sometimes difficult to find a great conversation on television today. But examples still exist, and one of my favorites is Charlie Rose.

Rose has been on TV a long time and has developed what is now a unique style of interviewing — one that encourages conversation rather than sets up sound bites. He attracts many serious thinkers to his show in part because he does not seek to catch them in a gaffe, but rather to offer them time and space to explain their thinking to a television audience.

Watching Charlie Rose is watching a great conversation leader work his craft. The Rose set makes it clear that the conversation is the most important part of the show — there's no fancy set or holograms or touch-screen graphics. It's the table and the guest and Charlie leading the conversation.

Perhaps more than other television interviewers, Charlie Rose uses conversation rather than interrogation. Rose's critics even say he talks too much in his interviews. But this is how the mood shifts from a volley to conversation. Guests aren't simply responding to incoming questions from the host — they are drawn into the conversational experience. It is all the more revelatory for the viewer. A Charlie Rose episode is a true exploration of a topic. Conversation — not interrogation — makes that possible.

Rose achieves this level of conversation with three key skills:

Persistence

It's a conversation, to be sure, but he's still leading the process. He does not attack, but he also keeps his guest on the topic at hand. It's a subtle method — a far cry from the yelling and cross-talking taking place over on the competition's shows. It is a beguiling process that draws the guest into an intimate space and encourages a frank discussion of the facts at hand.

Time and space

The world seems to move by at a faster pace than ever, with interviews now in increments of minutes. But Charlie Rose still takes the hour. And holds it. As reported in a 2009 *Fortune* profile, President Bill Clinton once agreed to a twenty-minute interview with Rose, and he held out for the full hour. Eventually, he got it. By insisting on the time, he keeps the potential for in-depth conversation to occur.

Personal involvement

Most shows engage a team of booking agents to secure guests. A 2009 *Fortune* profile notes that Charlie Rose is known to invite his guests himself. And this takes his art of conversation to its most personal style. With a personal touch, he encourages the guest to come on the show and converse.

Learning from Jamie Dimon

James "Jamie" Dimon is the CEO of JPMorgan Chase. He was named to *Time* magazine's list of the world's 100 most influential people four times. Watching him work is a study in the value of direct, fact-filled communication. He takes on tough issues, he faces the conversation head-on, and he backs up his statements with relevant facts. His clarity and his simple, straightforward language are his hallmarks, and he creates an air of instant credibility.

The Surprising Role Models

Finally, in my discussion of conversation tutors, I want to encourage you to look in unexpected places. Often where you see an individual making a tremendous impact in the lives of others, you will find a conversation leader. But these leaders are not always in the spotlight. They may be acting in ways that do not bring them a lot of attention and put them in the limelight. They are hard to spot. But when you see one, the opportunities to learn are substantial.

I had that experience recently when I was able to observe the workings of Alcoholics Anonymous in action. I had long known about the organization, of course, but when I was supporting the recovery of people close to me, I was able to see firsthand what brilliant use this group makes of conversation leadership. Members of Alcoholics Anonymous are individuals engaged in conversation to save lives. It is the highest use of the tactic, and I learned so much from seeing it up close.

The group uses conversation as a framework. When an individual enters the AA program, he or she does so in concert with a sponsor. The sponsor is not there to lecture or teach or monitor. Instead, the sponsor is there to start an ongoing conversation between the two of them as they move forward in recovery. They engage one another, they share and support one another. And between them, always, is the connection of dialogue. Back and forth, all the time, dialogue becomes the lifeline that each holds on to for the other.

It's only through exchange and dialogue that this process works. If one person stops talking, the conversation ends and the connection is lost.

I also had the opportunity, over time, to view counselors at work in the process of supporting recovery. This, too, was a true opportunity to see conversation at work at its highest purpose. Skilled counselors don't lecture or criticize or berate. Instead, they engage the hurt individual and lead that person forward with an exchange of emotional communication. This is a conversation that can create a pathway for an addict to move forward and reset his or her life.

Great conversation leaders exist all around. The opportunity to learn from them is right in front of us. The key is to spot the leaders and look for ways to observe them in action. Watch the conversation unfold, look for ways the leader uses words, body language, eye contact. Look for leaders in unexpected places.

LEADERS IN CONVERSATION: THE COUNSELOR

Vince Casalero is a friend and counselor I have spent time with in a variety of settings: as a personal adviser, socially, and, in some cases, when he was working with families to which I am close. My conversations with this particular counselor often echo in my head. He reminds me how powerful a tool honest conversation can be.

In one particular exchange we had, I was recounting an incident in my youth that I was ashamed of. I was having difficulty telling the story.

The counselor suggested that I reframe the incident. We all feel shame sometimes, he said. But sometimes these incidents can be very funny. Step outside yourself, think about how funny that was from another perspective. Give yourself the opportunity to see it as funny and erase the shame.

That was good advice. It was advice that worked for me and advice I have come back to many times in my life when the voice in my head starts messing with me.

But the other thing I learned from this encounter was how the counselor was able to bring me to that place. He didn't just jump out and tell me what to do. The advice part of the conversation came much later. The real work he did came up front—when he said very little. He led by listening.

This is a powerful experience that I have replayed in my head many times. I have come to recognize that a great conversation can take time to unfold. As the leader, you have to be patient. You have to listen and wait for the moment when your portion of the dialogue can be heard and accepted by the other person. An individual in pain wants to talk—and wants to be heard. It is a slow-motion conversation, but it is one that can have a powerful effect for years to come.

AFTER WORDS: ASK FOR NEW LEADS

There's an old salesman's trick I like to use in conversation leadership situations: I ask for new leads. Often we think we know who the movers and shakers are in our business circles. We may think we have our conversation wish list all planned out. When you ask, "Whom else should I be talking to?" you might be surprised by the answer you receive. This section will review my tactics for using one great conversation as a jumping-off point for the next great conversation.

I had an experience at an event once when I found myself in a conversation with Leslie Moonves, the CEO of CBS. We were having a casual executive-esque conversation, talking about the state of the marketplace, trends in marketing, and advertising. It was standard fare. And then I asked him: Whom else should I be talking to?

He didn't hesitate, proceeding to tell me about CBS Outdoor president Wally Kelly, who was responsible for outdoor advertising—a guy with a whole lot of billboards to fill.

"You should talk to him and see if the two of you can work together," he said.

We did. And the results were powerful. We ended up doing a deal with CBS Outdoor in which we launched and marketed a new product exclusively via CBS Outdoor advertising. It was a great success for us at retail and also a great success for CBS because it created such a strong case study in the power of their outdoor ad space. With no other advertising for that product, all the credit for the marketing power went to the CBS Outdoor platform.

And it all came from that one conversation.

NEXT STEPS: ALWAYS ON

Have your one-line conversation starter ready and waiting. Anytime is a good time to start a conversation and see where it leads. I have a whole host of favorite opening lines, from "Tell me about your company" to "Where do you come from?" to "You must be the one giving [insert boss's name here] so much trouble!" I use them with all manner of individuals: those who work for me, my peers, and those who outrank me.

McCANN'S PRINCIPLE NUMBER SIX: NEVER STOP LEARNING

Teachers are all around us. There will never be a moment when you can confidently say, "I know all that I need to know."

7

Global Conversations

W<small>E LIVE IN A WORLD</small> no longer constrained by physical borders.

This is not just a realization of the way digital technology has affected our communications. It is a recognition of the changed way we all view the world we live in. In previous generations — really not that long ago — it was customary to think of the national market as your main focus and the international market to be a reach goal. Companies that were able to expand into international markets were considered to be playing on an entirely different field.

Today, of course, that view of the world has changed. No one goes into business expecting to thrive and grow in his own little backyard. Doing business on a global level is not the sign of an unusually successful company — instead, it's a sign that a business has a pulse. Everyone has to look at the global marketplace.

How, then, can the conversation strategy we've been discussing play out on the global stage? Certainly, it's challenging. When you engage in a conversation across traditional national borders, you run into all kinds of new hurdles — language, culture, time zone, logistics. These are not easy conversations to have. But they are vital. As we all move beyond our initial borders and into the global mix, we have to be able to connect and form relationships. This is a process that cries out for conversation leadership. It's the best way to create the enduring, robust relationships that will allow all of us to grow and thrive in the international space.

In this chapter, I'll discuss the ways I've taken my philosophy of conversation leadership global.

Support Global Commerce

The first step in the process is the most obvious — it's the one that customers demand. Over the years, 1-800-Flowers.com has taken global its ability to receive and fulfill orders. We work with providers all over the world to make that happen — and there was no question that we had to. Customers don't think of themselves as confined by lines on a map. In today's era of mobile humanity, we have customers who want to send flowers to family back home on another continent. We have customers who want to thank their clients in different time zones.

In addition to the vendor relationships, we offer our customers information they need to be successful when sending internationally, such as international gift-giving do's and don'ts. For instance, if you decide to send flowers to Europe, ensure that the bouquet has an odd number of flowers in accordance with tradition.

We even have an international holiday and event calendar. Want to know the big gift-giving holidays in Brazil? Japan? Australia? This is an easy way to keep track.

And it's all designed to facilitate the conversations that customers want to have with global recipients.

When we think about our goals for global expansion, they are similar to the mission we've always been on in the U.S.: To deliver smiles. That smile is the connection we've facilitated between the sender and the recipient. When we can do that on a global scale, we make the world a smaller and more intimate place. We create, through our network of vendors and partners, a way for people to connect across oceans and time zones and cultural divides.

Create Global Business Partnerships

Creating a network of fulfillment partners around the world allows us to do business in more than 150 countries. Which is great. But we have not stopped at that level. Ultimately, our goal is to be the largest provider of flowers and gifts worldwide. And we want to one day have the ability to have the direct-ship and same-day capabilities in major markets that we do at home. This takes us into new territory — literally. This requires us to move beyond business arrangements and into business partnerships.

As the global marketplace has become more of an imperative for business, we have begun looking for partners and investments around the world. We haven't approached this global expansion tactically — listing countries to enter and then marching forward. Instead, we've looked for the opportunities that will give us the chance to have ongoing connections and conversations across time zones.

One of our most interesting global efforts is unfolding in Brazil. There, we have made a minority investment in the Brazilian family-owned business Flores Online. In many ways, this deal has all the hallmarks of the conversation leadership process I have so come to value in my work. The opportunity for the investment came to us via a conversation I had with Carlos Miranda, a leader in the private equity space, who knew of Flores Online and thought it would make a good investment for both his firm and ours.

On his advice, we explored the opportunity and made visits to Brazil to better understand the company and its goals. One of my most memorable conversations in that trip came when I spoke at dinner with the matriarch of the family — a woman who had spent her entire adult life working in the family floral business as a designer. In talking with her, I learned that she never wanted her firm to pursue the funeral business. The idea of her flowers at a funeral made her sad — she never wanted her artwork to be surrounded by sadness, only happiness.

From a business perspective, this was baffling. Had I been sitting back in my office in the U.S. learning of this odd rule this woman had, I might have discounted it as silly. But sitting there, talking to her, I could understand her passion for her artistry. I could see that this was not just a business to her, but an artistic calling.

This was my chance to talk to her about why I was in the flowers business. I could relate to her desire to deliver only smiles. That's certainly always been my mission. But, as I told her, smiles are not present in just times of joy. Sometimes it is in a time of sadness that you most need a smile. This is the job we can do together, I told her. This is the way your art delivers smiles, not just in times of joy, but also in times of sorrow — when a smile seems furthest away.

I'm still surprised I convinced her. It was a moment when I realized that even as I engage in global business, the usefulness of conversation is never far from reality. When you can connect, person-to-person, all kinds of new things are possible.

Through conversation, we were able to expand our business and theirs. It's a partnership that continues to bloom for all involved.

We made another minority investment in the UK — and this one couldn't be more different from our partner in Brazil.

In the UK, we went looking for a partner because it was a market we hoped we could penetrate. We found a firm called iFlorist, which boasted a network of nearly 2,000 florists and flower shops in the UK. When we made contact with the company, it was already delivering to dozens of countries around the world. Delivering flowers within four hours across the globe has given the company a reputation for quality and service. The company was granted the opportunity to present an exclusive floral bouquet to Queen Elizabeth II in honor of Her Majesty's Diamond Jubilee. But it was also a very young company, founded in 2006. While Flores Online was all about the art and beauty of flowers, iFlorist was all about their digital underpinnings. Their passion was code. And this proved to be a great place for us to begin a global conversation.

What struck us as we explored working with iFlorist is that this code was so beautifully designed for the global conversation. The company was at work only in the UK when we first made contact. But its transactional software was primed for far bigger things. It was set up to do business in any currency, to communicate in any language, to work across time zones. It was a staging ground for a global digital conversation. Did iFlorist love flowers the way our Brazilian matriarch did? No. But that didn't matter. This was a company that understood, as we did, that technology could facilitate strong relationships across time and space and language.

A third recent effort took us to Canada. We had long done business in Canada, but we were concerned that our initial partner was not in a position to grow with us. We looked for a new Canadian connection and found What A Bloom. In many ways, this new partner reminded me of me. The company CEO's vision was 100 percent entrepreneurial. We were a cultural fit.

Often I am asked which country I'll go into next. The answer is: it depends on where the conversation takes me. I don't look at global expansion as a country-by-country roll. Instead, each arrangement has its own reasons and its own value to the broader global conversation I want to support. When we look for a partner abroad, we look first at the financials — does a deal make business sense? And then we look for a cultural fit. As was the case of our partnership with What A Bloom, the cultural connection may be a passion for entrepreneurial process. With What A Bloom, a corporate cultural passion for technology connected us. And with Flores Online, it was a family business connected to the beauty of flowers that made us feel at home. In each of these cases, the relationship made the deal. If we cannot converse, we can't move forward, no matter how good the numbers may look on paper.

Create Global Employee Conversations

One of the great benefits of global partnerships is how they enrich the experiences of those of us back at the home office. Twice a year, for example, we hold a meeting of senior managers. People come together from all over the country and, now, from all over the world. The addition of our international partners takes the meeting to new levels. We are able to hear new ideas and exchange new information. Individuals who work for 1-800-Flowers.com see their own work in a new light—in the service of not just a domestic brand but also an international brand. The fact that we can create and support this global employee conversation means we can set the stage for new and bigger ideas.

LEADERS IN CONVERSATION: THE GLOBAL VIEW

Maria Dinelli of Ernst & Young invited me to speak to an audience in Saudi Arabia. I went to give my outlook on entrepreneurialism, and I ended up in a conversation that changed my outlook on the region.

After I spoke, I was at dinner with some of the participants, and one of them engaged me in a conversation about doing business in the Middle East. We need more companies that can foster entrepreneurial spirit in this region, he said. There is a lot of discussion by politicians and by government leaders about how peace can come to fruition in the Middle East. The answer, he said, may lie not in a political solution but in a business solution. What if, he said, the answer were to foster small business development in such a way as to encourage those living in the Middle East to seek peace—peace for business reasons. The way to involve individuals in this process is to create opportunities for entrepreneurial growth.

Like flower shops.

It was a powerful conversation that was still ringing in my ears as I returned home. We have not made a deal in the region yet—but the conversation was a catalyst for our exploring our options and potential opportunity. The impact of that conversation is ongoing.

AFTER WORDS: BRIDGING THE TIME ZONES

Global conversations can be harder to sustain. You don't have the daily contact you might with a domestic employee or vendor or even customer. So that makes follow-up even more vital in this context. If you're engaged in conversations across time zones, across international borders, or across languages, make the additional effort to respond, engage, and continue. Close the distance between you.

NEXT STEPS: TAKE OFF

This one is easy. Want to have global conversations? Get out and explore the globe. As wonderful as digital communication can be, it can never fully replace the feeling of sitting down to dinner, meeting for coffee, or gathering at a conference in another country. This is where real conversation can happen. Your screen will not suffice.

McCANN'S PRINCIPLE NUMBER SEVEN: THE WORLD IS OUR JOB

Business has a role to play in the global conversation. We are not bystanders in geopolitical events. We are part of the matrix that knits humanity together. We belong in the debates that shape our world.

8
—

Conversations with Community

I N MY OLD NEIGHBORHOOD in Queens, we always knew how things were going with our neighbors. You knew who was doing well, who'd had good news recently, who had reason to celebrate. At the same time, you also heard the chatter on the downside: whose business was faltering, whose children had trouble with the law, who was in need of a helping hand. You knew because word got around the neighborhood in a quick and predictable fashion. Deliverymen chatted with their customers. Housewives talked across fences. Grocers picked up the latest from vendors. It was a close circle of intensely local conversation. If you ran a business in the neighborhood, you knew what was going on just by listening to the conversations.

This continued as a legitimate process for me even as I started my own floral business. I spent time in my shop. I spent time in the neighborhood where my shop was located. I talked to everyone who came in and everyone I saw around the neighborhood. It was a familiar process for me.

But as my business grew larger, it naturally outgrew the street-level conversations that I and my father and my old neighborhood relied on. This is a common ailment that falls over successful businesses. They outgrow their local conversations. They grow out and up and into tall office towers and suburban office parks, and they stop hearing about the local gossip. They become cut off from the conversations — which are still happening, just not in their earshot.

I've spent a great deal of time and effort to ensure this does not happen to 1-800-Flowers.com — and in the process I think I've come up with some guidelines other large businesses can follow. I've learned over the years that if you want to stay in touch with community conversations, you have to be on a constant lookout for new and creative ways to be seen and heard and involved. Too often "community involvement" for a business is just another term for charity. It's an expectation that the big business will write a check — and that's it. I want our community involvement to go beyond just cash and be a force and a platform for the community conversation — the daily chatter that keeps us all connected and reminds us of who we are and why we're here.

As a CEO, I view my role as someone who shapes consensus and makes decisions with not only the shareholders in mind, but also the vendors, distributors, and staff. To be sure, my process is capitalist. But there's no reason that those of us who call ourselves capitalists can't embrace the growing movement around caring capitalism. It's a model that's made this country great. It's at work in great companies such as Whole Foods. And it's a natural fit for a firm such as ours. 1-800 Flowers.com is dedicated to helping customers express themselves and connect to the important people in their lives. We create smiles every day, from the sender to the recipient. Our company growth is about making more and more people happy.

But that doesn't just describe our marketing model. It also creates a framework for how the business interacts with the community, and it's one that all business leaders can embrace. CEOs have to focus not only on their customers, but also on the people behind the product, from computer systems to the types of trucks products are shipped in to the look and quality of the product. We can and should extend our caring circle to the communities we are in. These are the places that we, our employees, our vendors, and our customers call home.

In this chapter, I'll review some of the ways 1-800-Flowers .com has developed to remain connected to and supportive of the community conversation all around us. I'll talk about the goals we have, the programs we've started, and the way we try to shape our business so that we are always part of the conversation around the community. When you get to be a certain size, keeping up the community conversation takes more than an open door and a pot of coffee. You have to get creative.

Our Philanthropic Efforts

"Why not start our own charity?"

My brother Chris started this internal conversation in 2011. For many years, we as a company had been involved in many wonderful charitable efforts. We worked with organizations raising money to support breast cancer research. We have been part of programs devoted to education, food pantries, and many other wonderful and worthy efforts.

But was this our best effort? Was this the best and most robust way to connect to our community?

We began tossing around the idea of creating our own charity. We call it a philanthropic initiative — not program, since the word "program" suggests the effort has an end point. We see this not as a single event or even a single effort. It is a new way we've developed to connect with our communities and stay involved in the conversations they are having.

The initiative is called Imagine the Smiles. Here's how it works: We reach out to our communities and ask them to suggest recipients. We ask them to tell us — via letters or e-mails or social media — about someone in their community who they feel needs a "pick-me-up." It's a tremendous experience to then listen to what comes back. We hear all kinds of wonderful stories. We hear stories of extraordinary heroism — someone who literally saved a life or acted above and beyond the call of duty to help another person. And we hear stories about the everyday heroes — moms who go above and beyond for their children, teachers who are inspirations in the classroom, neighbors who help each other out without any expectation of recognition or reward.

From these nominations, we convene a panel of 1-800-Flowers .com employees. They review the applications and the stories and make decisions as to whom we as a company should grace with a surprise delivery of flowers and a featured spot on our website devoted to Imagine the Smiles.

They have a hard job! Among the great stories we've been part of so far:

I would like to nominate Brian F. In 2008, Bernie's Book Bank founder and executive director Brian Floriani left his job as a golf professional to become a reading paraprofessional for Shiloh Park Elementary in Zion, Illinois. The sudden death of his father, Dr. Bernard P. Floriani, for whom Bernie's Book Bank is named, inspired him to do something different with his life. Brian spent every day working with struggling readers. While he was able to help each one individually, he realized that his efforts were not doing anything to prepare young readers to enter school.

After learning that only 24 percent of incoming six-year-old children in Waukegan, Illinois, interacted with books, Brian began to envision a business that would pour children's books into at-risk homes, and help prepare children to enter school "reading ready." He began collecting children's books in his garage and distributed them in age-appropriate bags to children at Shiloh Park Elementary, and thus Bernie's Book Bank was born. Today, Brian is confident that Bernie's Book Bank can and will transform the educational journeys of at-risk children throughout America. He is thankful for every person who has helped us connect children needing books with books needing children. Brian and Bernie's Book Bank deserve all the smiles they can get for providing so many themselves.

Eileen, my wife, deserves a smile. She's a hard-working wife & mother and sole provider for our family. She's devoted, attentive, and available both at home and at the office. No one knows how she pulls it off. Thanks, honey!

I would like to nominate someone whom I haven't seen in thirty years. Her name is Shelly. We went to high school together on Bainbridge Island. We started planning our thirty-year class reunion two years ago and reconnected. We talk on the phone constantly but have yet to have our girls' day that we keep talking about. Shelly lost her job (which she desperately needs) just this last Tuesday. She needs a hug, and because I can't be there to do that, a gift of flowers would certainly brighten her day and let her know how much I appreciate her friendship and cannot wait for our girls' day.

That's just a sampling. We keep the stories coming on our Facebook page, and whenever we can we add a picture. This allows us to participate in this good moment and then share it so that anyone who clicks on it can see it as well.

This is a nice thing for us to do — give flowers away to folks who very much appreciate them. We've never gotten a picture back from one of these deliveries that did not show everyone involved wearing a great big smile. But how does this further our goal of community conversation? Honestly, it's not hard to see how this initiative sparks intense, widespread, robust discussion.

It gets our customers talking to us. When we first asked for nominees, the response was immediate. The in boxes and comment pages flooded with suggestions. In this day of cluttered media, everyone has a story he or she thinks should break through and be noticed. When we offered up our media platform for these stories, the storytellers were ready and eager to tell us what we wanted to know. It's never hard to ferret out the great stories in any community. You just have to offer the storytellers a chance to get up and tell what they know. You'd be surprised just how committed customers can be about making sure we get the information. We once had a gentleman who lived in Florida but wanted to nominate an individual he had seen on the news — a woman who had been instrumental in saving the lives of two children. The gentleman didn't know the woman's address — only that she'd been on the news. But he kept after our headquarters staff until we were able to track down the news story — and the woman — to deliver the bouquet.

It gets our customers talking to each other about their communities. When you're going about your daily life, it's hard sometimes to see the good that is going on all around you. The burdens of the day and the bad news that seems to fill the airwaves take over. Imagine the Smiles highlights the good for all of us to see and appreciate. We can share among ourselves the good news in our communities — our local communities or the wider human community. When someone is doing something good, it does us all good to hear about it.

It gets our employees talking. Why have an employee panel? It would be easy enough to have the nominations run by some Flowers staff in the communications department. They are all good people and are perfectly capable of picking a good candidate from among the nominees. But instead we opened the program to all employees and gave them the chance to sit on this panel, be part of this conversation between us and our customers, and take the opportunity to give back to these individuals: Great job. We're proud of what you've done and we're happy to acknowledge you.

Imagine the Smiles was an immediate hit with employees, and we have a multimonth waiting list to get onto the decision panel. We've also instituted a policy whereby new employees will be assigned to participate in the monthly panel soon after they come on-board. This experience, I believe, gives newcomers a clear understanding of who we are as a company and how we want to interact with the community around us.

It also lets us set up future conversations. The process of awarding the bouquet is often one that creates a first connection between a customer and one of our local florists. Although it's our brand name that everyone sees, our bouquets are fashioned and delivered by local florists — working members of the community. That's who ultimately fulfills the request for a bouquet and that's who completes the final mile of the initiative. That's the store where the bouquet will be arranged, that's the local delivery guy who will drive it out to its final destination. That's the connection we foster and that we hope will be the basis for more conversations in the future.

Imagine the Smiles is just the latest way we've developed to foster and participate in conversations with our community. Many of our charitable efforts revolve not around just the "free stuff" that often comes with a giveaway, but around the connections that they foster.

We also support an ongoing program called Cell Phones for Soldiers. 1-800-Flowers.com establishes cell phone collection points. The phones are recycled by a firm called ReCellular. ReCellular pays for each recycled phone — enough to pay for one hour of talk time for soldiers stationed far from home. That's an obvious conversation support effort.

Another of our charitable programs, more focused on the 1-800-Flowers.com community than the others, is called Cookies for A's. Our subsidiary Cheryl & Co. — a maker of fresh-baked gourmet cookies, brownies, and cakes — has a great program to inspire kids to reach their full educational potential. The company runs the popular Cookies for A's program and gives out free cookies for each A (or highest mark on a grading scale) when students present their report cards at a Cheryl & Co. store.

Giving away cookies is nice. But what's better? Giving away cookies in such a way that families come down to the stores, kids show off their successes by presenting a good report card, store staff takes the time to *ooh* and *ah* and congratulate the young scholar — and maybe Mom and Dad for their support — and then come the cookies. It's the interaction between families and the stores that we know makes this a worthwhile effort. If the cookie came in the mail, would it have the same effect? Maybe not. Connection in the community is what makes the cookie so sweet.

Connecting Through Public Relations

Charitable efforts are the most obvious way we connect with our community, but it's hardly our only effort. Another is public relations. And this gives me the opportunity to tell one of the great stories in 1-800-Flowers.com history. Was it good for conversation? Oh yes. We'll be talking about this one forever. This is the story of how my brother Chris and I came to be featured on the television reality show *Undercover Boss*.

It wasn't my idea. In fact, initially I said no way.

I was approached by the producers and asked if I would consider participating in the show — and for those of you who may have missed it, *Undercover Boss* is a reality show in which the head of a company masquerades as an employee. Wigs, glasses, and other trickery are deployed. The show ends with the big reveal at the end and with the boss often learning a few important lessons about what really goes on down on the floor of his shop on a daily basis.

But I wasn't interested in a career in reality television. I said no.

Then I got a phone call from my agent — the individual whose job it is to get me into visible, positive public relations situations.

"Are you crazy?" she said. "Did you really say no? Call back and say yes. Call right now!"

She had immediately recognized that this wasn't about me and what I wanted in my career. It was about a new way the 1-800-Flowers.com brand could make a connection with consumers — a very large audience of consumers.

I took her advice and called back, and we did in fact do an episode of *Undercover Boss*. But I convinced the producer that I was not the right person to play the lead undercover role. After all, I'm the guy who had his face on the side of a bus for more than a few marketing cycles. I'm far too recognizable — the gig would be up in the first five minutes of the show. Instead, I convinced them to use my brother Chris. As a part of the deal, I agreed to show up and surprise him on the job when he was undercover. (A chance to give my brother a dig was clearly a bonus — I was all in.)

The show was a great success in a number of ways — it was a chance for Flowers to boost its brand visibility in this television context, it was a chance to put Chris into the spotlight in a leadership role, and it was a chance for me to sneak up on him when he was trying not to attract attention and give him a hard time (which was the best part of the experience, no question). But beyond all those positive outcomes, the show did for us now what my face on a bus did for us years ago — it created a conversation point for the public to interact with our company.

Well after the show aired, we still get comments and feedback and discussion from people we've never met. In fact, I can often tell when the show has aired in reruns someplace because contact from the public spikes. People will call us, e-mail us, and post on our social media platforms to tell us what they thought about what they saw. And even if they don't reach out to us directly, they talk among themselves about the show — about the young franchisee we featured alongside Chris, the story of his efforts to move up in the business, and his making a place for himself in the industry.

And this, perhaps, is a key lesson in the way public relations plays a role in community conversations. Of course, efforts like this are undertaken to build a brand. When you're in business, you go on television to promote yourself, promote your company, and promote your brand. That's the goal of a lot of PR. But when you can find an opportunity like *Undercover Boss,* you can go beyond promotion. People didn't just hear about us. They talked about us. They're still talking.

Connecting Through Conscious Capitalism

I was invited by Doug Levy, a master conversational leader, to a gathering of executives at the offices of John Mackey, the founder of Whole Foods. We talked about many things we hoped we could accomplish in the world — initiatives around fair trade, environmental responsibility, and economic growth. All of us had a variety of different ideas floating in our heads, but what John Mackey helped us to see was the framework that all of us fell into: the matrix of Conscious Capitalism.

It's arcane to place the presence of social consciousness and capitalism at opposite ends of the human conversation. There is no reason they can't be joined. There are many of us in capitalist businesses who see that as part of our mission.

We face a host of enormous challenges in the world today — everything from climate change to hunger to economic turmoil. It's not possible for any one entity to solve problems when they reach this scale, but it is still our responsibility to participate in the solutions — particularly in the discussions around new and better solutions that might be developed.

Among our efforts:

As responsible global citizens, 1-800-Flowers.com is committed to helping to provide a sustainable environment for generations to come. From our corporate headquarters and support offices to our manufacturing and distribution facilities, our retail stores, our vendor choices, and throughout our supply chain, we are endeavoring to minimize our environmental footprint in a "green" and renewable fashion. Among the ecologically sound practices we employ are efforts to reduce waste, use energy efficiently, conserve natural resources such as water, and recycle whenever and wherever possible.

As noted on our company website, this commitment goes beyond our flowers business and into the other areas in which we sell. Fannie May Confections works very closely with our international cocoa suppliers and has long been a member of the National Confectioners Association (NCA), based in Washington, DC. We are active members of NCA's Chocolate Council, which works closely with the World Cocoa Foundation. As such, we actively support our suppliers and the work of these international organizations toward raising the standard of living for cocoa farmers and their communities worldwide.

I've also looked for ways to address the issues facing communities struggling through economic turmoil. As a part of our community service over the years, we have started a satellite business we call the Flower Barn. This is a business unlike any other we operate, because it employs the disabled. The concept was inspired in part by my own family situation. My brother, Kevin, is developmentally disabled. He will never live on his own or function independently in society. But in the right environment, he is able to work, have colleagues, contribute to a greater goal, and enjoy what we all enjoy in our work lives — the feeling of accomplishment that comes from a job well done.

It was that concept of the Flower Barn that got me thinking about other ways we could contribute to communities. What if a flower business sprang up in a community reeling from economic hardship? What if that sense of accomplishment, success, and belonging could be offered to workers who had the ability to work but not the opportunity to show it? We are incubating this idea as we consider our role as conversation starters in the greater community. Could we create and grow a business model that contributes to struggling communities in a new and creative and positive way? That's a conversation I've started internally at Flowers. It's one I'm starting to have with others who have explored the possibilities of community renewal.

In many ways, conversation drives our community service efforts. It's never been just about giving money away — although everyone always likes that. Using our position and our resources to start, foster, and participate in the conversation of the community takes me right back to my younger days in Queens. When we can help make those connections that used to be so natural in small neighborhoods, we contribute to the greater good far more powerfully than if we just gave money.

When we are approached to support any good cause, we often look for the conversation opportunities. Is this a way we can connect with customers? Is this a way we can help customers connect with each other? Is this a way that the conversation in our communities — be they local or global — can be supported? If so, this may make sense for us. It's the community conversation that drives us all forward. In many ways, the world has not changed so much since I lived in Queens. Only the scope of the conversation has been altered. And that is both a challenge and an opportunity.

LEADERS IN CONVERSATION: UNLIKELY LEADERS

Sometimes when we think we are "doing good" we are helping ourselves as much as the person we are helping. Perhaps more.

I have had many conversations with an individual employed in our headquarters named Brian and I mention him often when I give speeches on the topic of leadership. Brian came to work for us via a program called Vocational and Educational Services for Individuals with Disabilities. His cerebral palsy affected his speech and he needed braces to walk. But it didn't affect his ability to succeed at the company.

When Brian came to work for us, he was barely out of his teens. He started out in the mail room, and his sense of humor became his ticket up the ladder. Soon he was trading jokes with everyone on the staff, including me. He became what some in the company like to call the office "cruise director," moving through the halls from department to department, delivering the mail and doing the thing we so value as a company: engaging other people and creating and fostering connections. He was once a shy young man but now is one of our most confident employees. When I want to know what's going on in another department, I know I can ask Brian. He's plugged in.

AFTER WORDS: THE NEVER-ENDING CONVERSATION

When you invite the community into conversation, you have to be prepared not only for *what* comes back, but *when* it comes back. As I mentioned earlier, we participated in the reality show *Undercover Boss*. And the conversation we started in that experience comes back to us at all sorts of unexpected times. When either Chris or I are recognized in public, someone may bring it up. When the show airs in reruns, we get e-mails asking us about something that happened in the show. It reminds me that community conversation isn't something you can control. You speak, and you may hear back now—or years from now—and people will still expect you to be listening and ready to engage.

NEXT STEPS: ALWAYS ON(LINE)

Use technology to facilitate community conversation. More and more, we look to technology platforms to engage with individuals and companies alike. Customers will be shocked if they can't find you on Facebook, can't connect with you via text, and can't follow your CEO on Twitter. These are the ordinary daily conversation platforms of the new generation of customers. If you are not engaging in virtual conversation, you are missing the chance to talk with this influential group.

McCANN'S PRINCIPLE NUMBER EIGHT: THE COMMUNITY CONVERSATION IS ONGOING

Conversation is going on in the communities around you. If you are not participating, you are more than quiet. To the consumer, you are aloof, even uncaring. Engagement is not just an opportunity, it's a demand.

9
—

Conversation as Currency

SOME PEOPLE ARE BORN knowing exactly what they want to be when they grow up. They can articulate it with their first words, they dress up in the garb for Halloween, and they impress all manner of adults with their focus and determination.

I was not one of those kids. Instead, I was one of the many who had to try on a series of situations, looking for the right fit. My résumé is, well, colorful. I've tended bar, counseled troubled boys, painted houses, and sold leisure suits. And those are just the highlights.

But in my search for a profession, I tried out one that I didn't pursue, and it still managed to be one of the single most influential experiences of my education. It came one spring when I was in college — pursuing (so I imagined at the time) the career path to becoming a cop.

It was the late seventies, and I was working a series of different jobs while attending college at CUNY–John Jay in New York. I was slogging through an introduction to psychology course when we were presented with a theory called Transactional Analysis (or TA for short). TA is an integrative approach to the theory of psychology and psychotherapy that was formulated in the 1950s and popularized well into the late twentieth century as a theory of personality and a system for personal growth and personal change. It is essentially the root of the "I'm OK, You're OK" school of therapy. But that's not the part of the lecture that I was most impressed by. What struck me, as I waded through these chapters and listened to the professor drone on, was the insight into why people do what they do.

TA tells us many things, and one of them is that human beings crave social intimacy. They want to be connected. They look for "strokes," that is, contacts, from other people. These can take the form of a compliment, a hug, a smile, or a word of praise. We want these things — we need them, as we do any of the elemental essentials such as food and water. We will seek them out and pursue them in all our activities.

This was one of the most influential things I'd ever been told. The realization that yes, this is true, we do spend our days and nights in search of social intimacy, was an "aha" moment that would resonate for me for decades to come.

When you think about it, it makes perfect sense. Of course human contact is what we spend most of our lives searching for, caring about, and worrying over. Have you ever heard anyone say, "I have way too many friends"? Of course not. We value our friendships. We admire people who have lots of them. Having many friends is a sign of success, and we aspire to it. Have you ever heard someone say, "Too many people care about me"? Again, of course not. We consider people with lots of love and support around them to be rich. It's where we all want to be. It is a core human motivation, and it knows no borders, no social class boundaries, no gender split. It is a baseline experience and motivation we all share, no matter who we are, no matter where we come from, no matter what we may do in our lives.

I did not end up taking that knowledge of human psychology out into the neighborhood to walk the police officer's beat. Instead, I took it into my life as a businessman. I began to understand this powerful human force as an undercurrent of business — all business. We were, I realized, living in what I now call the contact economy. The contact economy is a marketplace of goods, services, and relationships, and conversation is its currency. It is the landscape on which all businesses live.

When you take apart the human insight of TA, you see that people don't spend their lives in search of money and other material goods (although it may appear so sometimes). That's just an outer layer of human personality. Underneath whatever we do for money, we also do it for social intimacy and for contact. We crave it and we seek it. When a business can provide it, that business will soar. These are the businesses that understand and embrace the reality of the contact economy.

The contact economy has a clear physical manifestation. Think about the center of any town or neighborhood. Often there is a focal point around a business. It may be a grocery store — one like the one in my old neighborhood in which the owner kept a credit book and knew the fortunes of every family in the vicinity. It may be a coffee shop, where neighbors gather in the morning to share news and face the day. It may be a bar à la *Cheers* "where everybody knows your name." Those are businesses that thrive on not just what they sell but what they offer to their customers beyond goods or services. They create a physical space for connection.

Human beings, driven by their emotional cores to seek out this connection, find businesses like this and open their wallets in support. These are businesses that people learn to love. They become institutions in their neighborhoods. The locals who grow up and move away can still be tipped into nostalgic moments at the mention of these businesses — an ice cream parlor, a drive-in movie theater, a dance hall, a bookstore. No matter what they may have purchased there, what they remember, what they love, it is the human contact the business made possible.

Certainly that was my experience back in my early days in the retail business. I sold flowers. But my store offered more than pretty plants for sale. We brewed coffee and kept chairs in the store so that people would stop by, hang out, chat for a while, and then move on. We played our role as members of the contact economy. We were doing more than providing goods. We were stepping up to our roles as contact providers. It's why people stopped by, even when they didn't want to buy flowers. And it was why when they wanted to buy flowers, they bought them from us. People want more than stuff; they want to feel connected — in the words of TA experts, they want strokes.

We took that philosophy forward to each incarnation of our business. When we moved into telephone sales, we made a point of hiring warm, friendly, outgoing people who would take naturally to a strokes-oriented business model. When we went online we had the same goal — to be a place for contact, a vehicle for connection, and a player in this essential human search. We created partnerships with AOL and later with Facebook. We created our own online forums and discussions to keep the conversation going and create contact opportunities. We brainstormed for products that allowed our customers to participate in the contact economy. One we came up with recently is a five-dollar cookie. It sounds so small, but it's huge to our younger customers who want to be in the contact economy but can't always afford the price points a big floral arrangement can command. So while they can't afford a dozen roses, they still want to reach out and make a connection. We continually look for ways to make that happen.

The contact economy is not new, and its effect on business has many examples, big and small. How did shopping malls come about? It wasn't because stores needed the space. It was because customers craved the interaction a shopping mall provides. Think about why people flock to malls — they may say it is to visit a favorite retailer. But if you watch them after they arrive, you see their quest not for goods but for contact. Kids come to hang out with their friends. Seniors come to walk the halls for exercise. Families arrive to window-shop and hit the food court. Retail is just the construct for this popular gathering place.

The power of the contact economy goes beyond retail and into all aspects of marketing. What are the marketing campaigns that resonate? The ones that offer connection. Reach out and touch someone.

Interestingly, the contact economy is the driving force behind the rise of social media. Lots of pundits will try to tell you this is about digital advancement and other technological trends, but that's just the hardware side of the story. The reason social media is part of the digital revolution is because the contact economy is so vibrant. When you see a social media tool take hold, you can bet that there's a basic human connection being fostered by the shiny new invention.

Take Twitter. I confess, I didn't understand Twitter in the beginning. It seemed so shallow to me. Why did I need to know what you ate for lunch or what your fashion dilemma was in real time? What was the purpose of these tiny pieces of communication?

It took a night of dinner and drinks with some of the younger, more technically savvy members of my team to set me straight. And when they explained how Twitter functions, I realized what I'd missed. Twitter is a player in the contact economy.

I didn't really need to know what you are shopping for at the grocery store. Or the difficulty you are having picking the right dress for the evening. Or the way you feel after that missed call during the ball game. But when you send out your 140 characters, you connect with me. It's a virtual version of small talk. Perhaps I don't really need to know all that — but there are some people from whom those fragments of information will be welcome. Little messages from you, tossed over the virtual lines, reminding me that you are out there, we are all connected, we are thinking of each other, and we are fine. These are the hallmarks of the TA mind-set. They are the elements that we crave — the strokes and the human contacts that we seek out in all our days and nights. Twitter is just the latest way we act out this core human behavior. No wonder it became so popular.

And of course, Twitter is just one example of the social media explosion. The industry booms thanks to our human desire to communicate and make connections. I don't really need to know that you checked in at Applebee's or that you are the "mayor" of the United Airlines shuttle to Washington, but that tidbit of information makes me feel connected to the daily rhythms of your life. I perhaps have no vital need to see your book wish list or know what music is coming through your computer speakers right now, but when I know this, I am, in a small way, right there with you. Social media is hot because it gives us all kinds of new ways to be in contact. It's a marketplace evolution that speaks to the core of our humanity. Why wouldn't we embrace it? It's a brand-new way to do what we love.

Business that offer us the opportunity to have these TA moments are the ones that are the most successful over time. Consider, for example, the once-vibrant rivalry between Walmart and Kmart. Both businesses were similar big-box discount stores. The promise to the consumer was similar — low prices, big parking lots, basic dry goods. But one of those two companies made out a lot better than the other. And there are many reasons for that, but one of them, I'd argue, is the fundamental understanding that Sam Walton had about the power of human connection and contact.

From the early days of Walmart, stores were built on personal connection. Sam Walton himself was a visible figure in the running of the company — his visits to stores were moments of corporate celebration. And this human face carried over into the ways he reached out to customers. Perhaps one of the most enduring and visible contributions to the retail landscape is the Walmart greeter — the individual whose sole job is to stand at the front of the store, tell you hello, and welcome you to Walmart. Was there ever a more pure expression of the contact economy at work? The greeter gives the shopper nothing of monetary value — no tip on the sales, no inside knowledge of the merchandise, nothing. It's nothing but a greeting. But people love it, and retailers all across the marketplace have adopted it. Nowadays, it's not unusual to walk into a store selling shoes or electronics or T-shirts and experience the same "Hello. Welcome to our store." That's a fundamental expression of connection that Walmart made into a retail tactic.

Kmart, on the other hand, went into Chapter 11 bankruptcy and is now owned by one of its former competitors. Who says human contact has no monetary value?

That's far from the only example. The rise of Starbucks is another good one. Coffee is not hard to make, and it's been available for a long time at many retail locations. So why did Starbucks take off the way it did? Good coffee, to be sure. But Starbucks offered something else — it offered a neighborhood gathering spot. Meeting at the Starbucks became a regular part of many individuals' lives. Today, if you stroll into a Starbucks in your neighborhood and look around, it's likely you will see someone you know. In addition to selling coffee, Starbucks sells its spaces as places for connection. It might be a face-to-face connection — a meet-up for coffee. It might be a virtual connection — a chance to log on and check e-mail. But connection and contact are as important to the success of the business as caffeine is.

In the digital space, there are even more examples. Facebook was born as a way for college students to connect and engage. Today, it's a way for consumers all over the world to connect and engage. Individuals use it, businesses use it, leaders of revolutions use it. The platform takes the concept of connection to entirely new heights.

All this competition in the contact economy has inspired 1-800-Flowers.com to come up with new ways to stay current. We've found ways to offer strokes outside of the traditional customer transaction. For example, we developed our occasional necessity to say "no."

We are often asked to donate flowers to a charitable event. It seems like a small thing to ask of us, but if we said yes to every one of these requests, we'd go broke. We can't be in the business of giving away our merchandise on a regular basis. But at the same time, we hate to say no — especially to a good cause. So we've developed a process to address this ongoing issue that is straight out of the TA playbook.

Our most common request for free flowers often involves a local organization reaching out to its local florist. Here's what we do. The local representative says: We can't give away our flowers, but we'd love to help. Bring a dozen people from your organization down to our shop. We'll have some of our best designers come in and we can donate the workspace, tools, and know-how to help you all create centerpieces for your event.

The day of the event, the team comes in and we have our representative coach them through the process of creating great centerpieces. They aren't free, but the organization saves some money by doing the hard work itself. At the end of the sessions, the flower arrangements are complete, and everyone had a great time.

And now the TA part of the process kicks in.

We have a Flowers rep attend the event. At the end of the presentation, we have our Flowers rep take the mic and give a speech like this:

"We at 1-800-Flowers.com are delighted to be part of this event, but I have to tell you, the terrific centerpieces and other floral arrangements you see around you today were not the work of our designers. In fact, they were done by a team of rookies who had never done anything like this before. So I would like to hand out some certificates to recognize this group."

And then the Flowers rep reads off the names of all who participated in the flower arrangement party. We have a photographer take some pictures. It is always a warm and wonderful moment in the evening's events.

This is a classic TA-centric experience. We didn't hand out cash. We didn't give away merchandise. Our outlay of hard currency was quite minimal. Yet the impact of our efforts was substantial. We created a way for people in the organization to do something great, and then we recognized them publicly for their efforts. Everyone likes to hear their name announced over the PA system and walk up to the podium amid applause. It costs us little — far less than it would have cost to donate a bunch of centerpieces. And everyone is far happier with the outcome.

As the digital age continues to transform the economy, it's important to realize that change and flexibility will be a permanent part of the experience. The best way to roll with the changes is to keep the goal in mind: We are in business to provide connection. Whatever tool we use to make that happen is a worthy investment.

Still, investments change over time. For a while, we were very invested in Second Life, a virtual reality with a strong business presence. We contracted with an agency that specialized in Second Life marketing, we worked hard to develop a presence in the space, and we were successful in participating in this revolutionary digital experience. The intense consumer interest around Second Life lasted a few years, and then consumer eyeballs moved on to new options. This is to be expected, and it did not diminish our efforts. When the contact economy was in Second Life, we were there. When consumers went in search of contact elsewhere, we were part of that shift. Nothing is forever, and that's especially true in the digital world, where the pace of change is quick and constant. My goal is to be the best experience for the customer in any format — including the ones yet to be discovered.

Today, we see business moving into more visual digital formats such as Pinterest and Instagram. Like the platforms that came before them, these are essentially ways for individuals to make connections. Instead of connections made via short bursts of text, these are connections made through pictures and other visuals. Whatever format you choose, it's good old-fashioned TA at work. My psychology professor was right.

Understanding the contact economy goes beyond our customer programs. We who work here are also human beings, with the same needs for strokes and contact as everyone else. I look for ways to help Flowers employees connect and communicate, too. We invested in technology to make communication within the company more visual and more robust. But I also invest my own time and effort in the personal communication that makes working at a company worthwhile. About half my work life is spent on the road, and many of these trips are made to let me communicate with our staff and with our vendors — and to give them the chance to communicate with each other.

Here's an example: I led a two-day partner summit with our service center home agents and vendor partners from the Philippines and Central America. I don't see these people on a regular basis, and they don't always have a lot of contact with each other during the course of regular work process. This is an annual event for them. I gave a kick-off speech and then I opened the floor to free-form discussion. Flip charts went up all over the room and they were filled with ideas. Everyone in the room had three "votes" to put next to ideas. There are lots of ways to solicit ideas and feedback from employees — but when you can do it in a way that makes them feel connected and valued, you get the best and most innovative thinking. Everyone in the room responded to the desire to be connected to the discussion. The results were powerful.

We continually look for ways to help our employees not only benefit from the contact economy, but create their own contacts. Twice a year — in the fall and in the spring — we engage in a process of cross-training. We identify two dozen or so promising individuals and we rotate them into different positions for a day. Someone in accounting moves to customer service. An individual in the telecenter moves to IT. We'll even go up the food chain and have an executive swap chairs — perhaps someone from retails operations to comptroller.

This game gets harder to play as the company grows larger, but its benefit to the employees who get to play it is enormous. Yes, our key goal is to have each person learn about another individual's job. But there is a contact economy undercurrent to the day. Everyone who participates learns new skills, learns more about the wider operations of the company, and creates contacts. It is these contacts that will make teamwork possible down the road.

We want our employees to work as a team, so we work to make it possible. We could order them to do it. But we are far more successful when we understand how and why people mesh as a team. They don't do it for the paycheck or the bonus or even the promotion. They are often most motivated by human connection. Cross-training lays the connection groundwork for profitable teamwork.

When you embrace the basic human need for connection, many of your business decisions become clearer. Whether you are deciding on a new product, a new ad campaign, a new technology, or a new employee policy — ask yourself: Which way will best support the human need for social intimacy? Your answer to that question should be your guide. I learned that a long time ago. I can't remember if I did well in that psychology class or not, way back when. I did not use the information as I thought I would. But it's never let me down since.

LEADERS IN CONVERSATION: MONEY TALKS

I was sitting at lunch at the annual media conference run by Allen & Company in July 2010, listening in on a conversation at my table.

Cory Booker, the mayor of Newark, was talking to two technologists, Mark Pincus and Reid Hoffman, about the changes the mayor felt were critical to turn around the struggling Newark school system. The changes couldn't just be incremental, Booker argued. They needed to be sweeping, massive, overpowering.

"A truckload of change," said Booker. "And that takes a lot of money."

Mark Pincus waved a hand at the next table, where Mark Zuckerberg, the founder of Facebook, was having lunch with some other conference goers.

"Mark has a lot of money," he said, chuckling.

"Yeah, go ask Mark," Reid Hoffman chimed in.

Booker sat for a second. Then he did it: he scooped up his plate of barbecue and three-bean salad and moved to the next table, sitting down next to Zuckerberg. I imagine the conversation went something like this:

"You know, if you're interested in pursuing some big ideas, I could discuss this with you," Booker said to Zuckerberg.

"I'm interested," replied Zuckerberg.

Many of you may already know what came out of that exchange. Those were the opening moments of what would eventually be Zuckerberg's $100 million gift to the struggling public school system of Newark, New Jersey.

So, what exactly did I witness that morning?

I saw a moment in which conversation became currency. Booker initiated the exchange on the hunch that Zuckerberg was a man to come to with ideas for radical change. Zuckerberg's receptiveness to the approach, let alone the ensuing public gift, shows that he enthusiastically appreciated the proposition. What I witnessed was the brief, honest conversation that sparked one of the most important acts of philanthropy. This kind of interaction is the way great feats are accomplished.

AFTER WORDS: SAY WHAT YOU MEAN, MEAN WHAT YOU SAY

No stroke is a positive experience if it turns out to be a lie. When we interact with our fellow human beings and offer praise, warmth, understanding, and connection, we have to be ready to back that connection up with our actions. The customer service reps at 1-800-Flowers.com, for example, are trained not just to engage in a positive conversation, but to follow up and do what's necessary to make a customer happy.

NEXT STEPS: THE VALUE OF THE HANDSHAKE

In a digital age, it becomes easy to use the keyboard to connect. This is positive for speed and breadth of conversation, but it can come at the expense of depth. Half of my year, I am on the road so that my own contact economy does not slip entirely into the digital space. As much as I value the connections that digital communications can create, I work to maintain the face-to-face connections that got me started in the first place.

McCANN'S PRINCIPLE NUMBER NINE: TIME ISN'T MONEY; CONNECTION IS

Far too often we assume in business that the bottom line is the driver of all interactions. Everyone wants a great price, it's true. But everyone *needs* interaction and connection. Give the people what they need.

10

—

Talking Your Way Out of Trouble

I F YOU'VE EVER MET with a crisis communications team — a group convened to help you manage your personal or professional reputation during a crisis — you might have had the same realization I had: for professional communicators, they often put a very high value on silence.

Indeed, a meeting with a crisis communication team can be one in which you're advised to stop communicating. As the plan of action is formed, you may get the advice to hold your tongue. Don't talk to the media. Don't talk a lot around the office about what's going on. And above all — do *not* go out and try to talk to whoever is mad at you. Absolutely, positively no.

Crisis communications has its value, no question. But the advice to be silent is not one that I've found always works. In fact, there have been many times when I've found that a crisis is best solved with the opposite strategy — opening up the conversation.

In conversation, I've found, you can stop trading barbs and accusations and work toward real and valuable solutions. They are not always the easiest conversations to have. Many times, they are tense and uncomfortable, and everyone wishes he or she could be someplace else. But these are the conversations that fix things. These are times when conversations — if you're willing to do the hard work and endure the discomfort — can get you out of trouble.

In this chapter, I'll talk about how I've used conversation as a strategy to climb out of a hole — and how I feel strongly about teaching this skill to others and modeling it in my business dealings.

From 1-800-Flowers.com History

Not long after acquiring the 1-800-Flowers phone number, I discovered that the company I had acquired had no real assets, just debts and lots of them. It had nice offices in Dallas, with great modern furniture and beautiful views of the city — all of which had been bought on credit and none of which was actually owned by the company. With sales slow and 800 numbers still not well developed as an order channel for floral customers, I quickly realized that I had bitten off quite a bit more than I could chew.

In my eagerness to acquire the 800 number to create a new kind of retail company, I had not looked deeply enough into the company's financial condition. Most businesspeople are familiar with the concept of due diligence. But I was young and proud and sure of myself, and I didn't follow the rule book. My "due negligence" resulted in several million dollars in debts to vendors, landlords, suppliers, and, most important, florists, which would be difficult, if not impossible, to pay off based on the low volume of orders the nascent brand was generating.

As an entrepreneur with a small chain of retail floral stores in the New York City area, I was familiar with tight budgets and barely making payroll and rent at the end of the week and month. What I was not familiar with was how to manage millions of dollars in obligations while trying to build a retail brand and generate sales. I was faced with a capital crisis, one that was much larger and more complicated than any I had ever faced before. I was in completely new territory.

What to do? I did what I always had done throughout my business career — I reached out for advice. It's not what everyone would have done. Plenty of people might think that if you make a poor business decision, you should just keep mum about it and hope no one finds out. It's not uncommon to resort to reputation management when things are not going as planned. That way, things may be bad but at least no one knows about it. I respect that as a popular position, but I know enough to know that it wouldn't work for me. My whole career — really, my whole life — had been a series of interactions and relationships that had helped me see the way forward through good times and bad. If I was going to get out of this mess I had invested in, I was going to have to talk my way out. I needed some advice on how to proceed.

I reached out to my network of business associates for advice. Even at that early stage in my career, I had amassed many conversation partners, and I discovered that many were happy to take my call and discuss my situation. I spoke with bankers in Dallas and

New York. I called other florists around the country that I'd met over the years at industry events. I even chatted up retail shop owners in my own neighborhood — the local dry cleaner, the corner delicatessen, the hardware store, and the Laundromat operator. I was brutally honest about what I'd gotten myself into. I told them about the debt, my "due negligence," and my confidence — despite the financial mess — that I still had in the marketing power of the 1-800-Flowers concept.

Consensus from one and all was that I should declare bankruptcy, negotiate to pay pennies on the dollar to my debtors, and move on. "Hey," one said, "isn't that what the bankruptcy laws are for?" It seemed like sound financial advice and a very appealing way out from under crushing debt.

That is, until I had a conversation with my grandmother.

She listened to my tale of fiscal woe and considered all the sage financial advice I had received from various bankers and business owners, and then proceeded to, how shall I say it, "take me out to the woodshed." In no uncertain terms she informed me that McCanns did not welch on debts or use the courts or any other shortcut to fix our problems. We manned up and worked our way out.

And then she took the conversation beyond the financials, past the moral platitudes, and into the human element of the story. "What will happen to the florists — the storefront businesses — who have been struggling and wondering how all of this is going to work out? What happens to them when you go to court and come up with a deal that lets you walk away and leaves them with pennies on the dollar?" she wanted to know.

If that were not enough, she had one more point.

"These are the people you'll want to do business with in the future. How will they see you if you move ahead with a plan that saves you and hurts them?"

There was no quick, clean path out of this problem, she told me. We were all in this together.

All of these points should have been obvious to me, but sometimes it takes a mom to provide some clear business logic. So instead of filing for bankruptcy, I met with each and every one of the people and companies to whom we now owed money and laid out my business plan. I traveled to many of these businesses personally. I sat in flower shops that were just like mine on First Avenue — small, neighborhood-based, intimate operations committed to bringing smiles every day to the people around them. Many of these were mom-and-pop operations. They were the kind of businesses that keep a neighborhood humming. And I was in town to tell them just how badly the vendor they'd partnered with had screwed up.

These were not easy conversations to have. The business had been in trouble for some time — I had sensed that myself when I was a vendor and not yet an owner. I was approaching people who were owed money and knew that it was possible they'd never see it again. And who was I, knocking on their doors? I was not a known quantity to many of them. There was no indication I had the cash to bail us all out. All I had was my plan. And my willingness to sit down with them and discuss it.

I told them that if they were willing to work with me, they had my personal promise to pay them in full. I talked about why I felt the vision I had for the brand was still viable — even though the previous owners had loaded it down with debt. I talked about my plan for growth and how I did not want to take the path of least resistance and let the bankruptcy court come in and wipe the slate clean. That alternative, as we all knew, would not benefit any of us. They wouldn't get most of their money. I wouldn't get the chance to build the business I was sure was trapped inside this mismanaged brand.

By the end of my talking tour, most of the florists had agreed to give me and my idea a shot. If I'd sent a letter — or a lawyer — many would not have even entertained the crazy plan I had in mind. Many added that it was my personal outreach and commitment to the business that swayed them. There were some who told me no. There were some who were simply fed up with the financial turmoil the company had created before I'd come along. And there were some who simply could not keep their business going while they waited for me to execute the new strategy and jump-start growth. For those who could not afford to wait, I scraped and borrowed enough to pay them back if not 100 percent, then as close as possible. With the rest, I resolved to move ahead.

Although we were not a big enough company at the time to generate much news coverage, my conversation strategy got around. Businesspeople talk among themselves, and certainly the many creditors of 1-800-Flowers and those who did business with them had a keen interest in what I might do next. I discovered later that my process of conversation rather than legal action quickly made its way around the industry and greatly enhanced the reputation of my young company. If I'd filed Chapter 11 and discharged my debts, would that have had the same positive effect on my reputation? Clearly not. It would have been legal. It might even have been financially advisable. But my conversation strategy put me in a new light with this business circle. My strategy suggested that I had a new and collaborative way of doing business — one that set me apart. My willingness to meet the creditors, talk to them, discuss the options, and then agree to an arrangement gave me an entirely new image in the industry. Conversation was hard. But it worked.

This is a lesson I've taken forward in my life, both professionally and personally. Certainly, it's the process that I insist my employees follow to resolve a difference with a customer — engage, discuss, work out a solution. Don't shy away from the conversation just because it might not be pleasant. I don't insist that my employees continue to engage with an abusive customer. Every once in a while, you get someone on the line who won't be made happy and just wants to bawl out the unfortunate employee on the other end of the call. When that happens — and it isn't very often, but it's not unheard of — my staff knows they have my permission to "fire" that customer. But it's not a regular occurrence, and more often than not, hanging in there, talking it out, and engaging in conversation can lead both parties to an agreeable resolution.

It's advice I give personally as well. A friend for whom I have great admiration found himself in a legal tangle. It was clear he had not behaved well, but it was also clear — to me at least — that the attack on him was out of proportion. He came to me for advice. His initial instinct was to follow the traditional crisis communication strategy: go underground, send his family away, hunker down and be silent.

I suggested another route. Instead of digging a hole and jumping in, I urged him to consider a conversational strategy to move out of a defensive mode. Such a strategy is not easy to execute.

163

Sometimes in legal situations there are things you just can't say without undermining your lawyers and their efforts to help you. But in this case, we were able to find a way that a new conversation, started outside the legal arena, was able to begin the process of moving my friend out of his hole. Instead of hiding from the events, he began to talk about the broader social situations that allow these types of events to emerge — the systemic landscape that breeds this sort of error. Let's talk about how to make changes so this doesn't continue to occur, he said. Let's talk about how we move from accusations to more permanent solutions.

Sometimes, I need other people to remind me of this advice when I'm the one under attack. When you're a CEO and visible, as I am, some people will take shots at you — perhaps to give themselves a business advantage or perhaps just to see what happens when they try. In a free society and in a free market, people are going to say things, and sometimes they are hurtful.

I'm human. When someone says something negative about me, it stings. This is true even after my many years of running a company, after my many years of consciously shaping my role as the public face of the company. You'd think I'd be used to it, or at least able to shrug it off easily. But not always. I had a recent experience in which I was the focus of negative press — and even after all my years in this job I was ready to call out the dogs and come back with a classic crisis PR response — angry, looking to take my detractors down a peg.

It took someone outside my circle to engage me in conversation and remind me of the strategy that had served me so well. Trading accusations and negativity never gets us anywhere. Engage, discuss, talk about the problems, and see what emerges as a possible solution. Tapping into the cooler heads around me, I was able to reconnect with the process I knew was the right one. There's no need to move into the classic crisis PR mode. Let's talk about this and see what we can come up with as a solution that works for all of us.

I continue to use this advice in all spheres of my life. A project I've taken on recently is my investment and involvement with the New York Mets. As a lifelong Mets fan, nothing would make me happier than to see them win every game from now until forever. But since that's not likely to happen, I've begun to engage my fellow owners in a conversation that I hope will contribute to a new era for New York baseball, one that is about the fans and the conversation, and less about the score of any given game.

As part of this process, I've engaged in and encouraged conversation at every level of the organization. I've talked to Fred and Jeff Wilpon and David Newman. I've set up meetings so that they can meet with people I've met in the event and entertainment industry. And I've begun talking about what kind of conversation we need to have with the fans. In an era of social media, it's perfectly possible to converse on a wide level with baseball fans all over New York. All of these conversations, I know from experience, will lead us forward.

The Mets have not been winning a lot, and that's something even a casual fan of the game can see. They've also had financial woes in recent years — also not hard to find out. But climbing into the hole and staying silent about these events won't make them go away and it won't make anyone feel better about the situation. The way forward, I believe, is the way that I proceeded after I arrived in Dallas and learned my brand-new investment was actually a big, fat, disastrous collection of debts. The way forward is through conversation — sometimes painful, sometimes enlightening — but always with the opportunity to find a new way ahead.

Will it work? That part of the story is still unwritten. Conversations that change institutions can take many years to produce results. I have a vision of a sports brand that offers an experience to the fans and the city that is so engaging and so rewarding, no one will care who wins the game. When you can go to the ball game with your family and have a great time and feel connected to the team and to the fans around you, the score is hardly the most important thing. This is possible, I believe. And it's what I want to talk about with all the members of the Mets community. Will everyone involved get everything they want? Maybe not. But everyone involved will know they are being heard — just like the 1-800-Flowers creditors. They will know their team reached out to them to talk about what to do next. Believe me, no one in New York is going to get an e-mail from the Steinbrenners asking for his or her advice and input. We will be creating a uniquely Mets conversation. Perhaps it will even be one that resonates in a wider way throughout professional sports.

In life and in business, crises will happen. No one's experience is smooth sailing all the time. But as my mother reminded me back in the first months of my capital crisis, hunkering down is not always the answer. When you can think about what makes the most sense for everyone involved and engage in conversation with them, you can together come up with positive solutions that benefit all. We have courts for a reason. They are useful when we can't work out our differences. But far too often, we fail to try. Conversation is not just chitchat, and that's certainly true in a crisis.

Instead of going straight to crisis communication (which is often essentially silence), try first a round of crisis conversation. See if that doesn't spark the necessary ideas that get everyone back on track and cheering again.

When the crisis hits, resist the urge to pull back, clam up, and stay out of sight. Be brave and move forward into the conversation. Someone out there may actually have your solution. You'll never know if you don't ask.

LEADERS IN CONVERSATION: MISSED OPPORTUNITIES

Here's a story about a conversation I should have had.

A few years back, I met a lovely and talented young woman named Clara Shih. I met Clara in Madrid after we had given back-to-back keynote speeches at a major business and technology conference. Her message that the social Web is not just new technology, it is a cultural movement, struck a chord with me. I've met and conversed with her many times since. She's a visionary in the social media space and has great ideas about how the new digital conversations are shaping the world. I even wrote the foreword to her book *The Facebook Era*. I feel even more excited about the Facebook Era than I did about toll-free numbers or the Internet. The social Web is about connecting with customers again, hearing their stories, and sharing in their joys and sorrows and the most important moments of their lives. It's about reopening the dialog so that businesses can put customers back in the driver's seat and keep getting better.

I suggested to my board members that we should invite her to join the 1-800-Flowers.com board. They didn't go for it. Some of the more seasoned members thought that she lacked the gravitas for board membership. I didn't agree. But I didn't press the idea.

Soon afterwards, Clara Shih joined a board: Starbucks.

I went back to my own board and apologized. Because frankly, I should have stayed in that conversation and pressed my point. When I didn't, I let the opportunity drop. Sometimes, conversations are difficult because they challenge old friends and colleagues. They suggest that something tried-and-true must now change. These conversations can be uncomfortable for all. But as I watch the talented Ms. Shih now grace the board of Starbucks with her wisdom and her insight, I'm reminded that however difficult it might have been to press the point then, it's a lot more difficult now to regret my silence. Clara Shih now plays a role in my life as a thought leader and as a reminder to speak up and speak out when times are changing around us.

AFTER WORDS: CREATING SYSTEMS

All companies develop systems, and over time 1-800-Flowers.com has come up with FAP—it stands for Follow-Up Action Plan. It's critical for making the most of any conversation, and it's especially important when the conversations are difficult and the stakes for finding a solution are high. In any conversation about a trouble spot, a part of your agenda should be to set a FAP in place. This is how you keep conversation moving you forward and not just filling up the room with hot air. It's also a concrete way to communicate to your conversation partners that you're not just chatting—this conversation is designed to produce a plan, action, and results.

NEXT STEPS: THE PERMANENT RECORD

Keep notes. After all meetings, I often take out a piece of paper from my jacket pocket and jot down a few notes. Over the years, my assistant Patty has become adept at reading my scrawl and keeping track of my jottings. The act of note taking has two goals: One, it ensures that the creative ideas of the meeting are not lost as the participants disperse and go on to other tasks of the day. And two, the act of committing a note to paper—or to an electronic device if that's your method—is a way to solidify the thinking in your own head. By putting it in writing, you make a more permanent place for the idea in your own memory.

McCANN'S PRINCIPLE NUMBER TEN: SOMETIMES, THE BEST OFFENSE IS A GOOD CONVERSATION

It is natural when under attack to want to circle the wagons and go into battle mode. But conversation with an outsider—an individual who can keep emotion out of the discussion and give you the perspective you need to make the best choice—may help you see a new way forward.

Epilogue

As a company, we've gone through four waves.

The first wave was retail stores. Many of our best ideas were born in that period. I often find myself thinking back to that stage to evaluate anything new that comes across my desk.

The second wave was the 800 number. I first had that idea one morning while shaving and listening to the radio. An 800 number that incorporates the name of the company — what a great idea! It seems so low-tech today to talk about a phone line as a business innovation, but it was one of the best things we ever did.

Betting on the Internet was our third wave. We were doing deals with AOL and CompuServe before anyone really understood how this whole Internet thing was going to play out. But it seemed like it might be big, and we were not the type of company to sit back and let others explore the new territory first. We were out in front, staking our claim in the new virtual marketplace.

And now we're on our fourth wave. It's all about social. All about mobile. All about local. The things we want in our lives and the way we view our technology are coming together to create new, vivid experiences for all of us as consumers and retailers.

I had a conversation once with Jeff Bezos, the CEO of Amazon .com. We were together at a professional event and we were talking about his next wave — the challenge of rolling out same-day delivery. After a few minutes, he stopped and said to me:

"Hey, you guys have been doing same-day delivery all along. Maybe we should talk to you!"

The world continues to change but the skills we have learned are still part of why we are successful. The systems we have developed to deliver smiles don't go away as each new wave breaks over the marketplace. We marshal them and use them as we find a way to improve upon what we do.

What's the next wave? Hard to say. But it is certainly coming. And I expect it will give us all a lot more to talk about.

Appendix
Conversations Resources

Some of the best things I've read that inform my strategy of conversation leadership:

From the Bookshelf

Purple Cow by Seth Godin
I like much of Seth Godin's work and find him an important and influential voice in the business world today. Godin says the only way to spread the word about an idea is for that idea to earn buzz by being remarkable. He calls a remarkable product or service a purple cow. Ads on television and radio are classified as "interruption marketing"—they interrupt the customers while they are doing something else. Godin introduced the concept of permission marketing, in which the business provides something anticipated and relevant. He's worth reading—in both book and online form.

Hierarchy of Needs by Abraham H. Maslow
This is a text I was introduced to in college—long before my business career took off. It has remained influential in my business life because it offered me a way to see human beings and their needs in a clarified and concrete way. It's

an eye opener for those of us in consumer marketing. It helps us to understand why some brands fail and others succeed. Often, it's not a question of how good the businessman is, but how well he has positioned his brand with regard to the psychological needs of his customer base.

If the original psychology text is too daunting, you might try sampling Maslow in some more business-friendly formats:

Maslow on Management by Abraham H. Maslow
Continuous improvement and empowerment are among the many current management practices that owe core elements to Maslow's principles. This text shows how many of Maslow's concepts have become bedrock to modern corporate tactics.

The Maslow Business Reader edited by Deborah C. Stephens
This collection of letters and essays by Maslow gives the reader a broad introduction to his breakthroughs on the topic of management. The texts are taken from both published and unpublished works.

See You at the Top by Zig Ziglar
This is the classic book from the great motivational speaker and expert on the power of human interaction. I knew Zig personally, and his ability to inspire and coach individuals toward positive change was remarkable.

In addition to *See You at the Top*, his most famous book, other great Zig books include:

Secrets of Closing the Sale
In this text, Zig Ziglar lets you in on his secrets:

- Successful closings for every type of situation
- Questions that will show you new possibilities you may never have considered
- Tips on how to "paint word pictures" and use your imagination to realize the results you seek
- Advice from top salespeople

Better Than Good
This text, collects Zig's stories from his half-century career as a speaker, au-

thor, and world-class motivator. Through these tales he helps the reader understand how so many have followed the Zig Ziglar teachings to overcome fear and failure.

Raising Positive Kids in a Negative World
In this text, Zig adapts his concepts for families and develops a simple prescription for dealing with kids.

Drive by Daniel H. Pink
Pink continues his practice of offering up keen observations of human motivation — this time in the workplace. His thinking dovetails with his other books that focus on the consumer marketplace. Pink's discussion of why we do what we do and his use of research to support his philosophy make his books relevant and important for any smart communicator.

Tribal Leadership by Dave Logan, John King, and Halee Fischer-Wright
We live and work in the modern age, but much of what motivates us has primal roots. In this book, the authors reveal the tribal instincts and habits that motivate work groups today. What's more, they examine the ways we can understand these behaviors, get groups to communicate, and come together for the overall corporate good.

The 7 Habits of Highly Effective People by Stephen R. Covey
Covey is a famed innovator in the leadership space. He broke new ground by maintaining that true success is a balance of personal and professional effectiveness. His book remains a classic instruction manual for those of us with big plans for life, business, and the marketplace but still just twenty-four hours in the day. Also worth reading: Covey's later work, *The 8th Habit: From Effectiveness to Greatness.* This text acknowledges the revolution of the digital era and the widespread changes that came with it. The book deals with the "new normal" of the technology age, and special attention is given to the demands and opportunities of the knowledge worker.

Growth in a Growthless Society by Robert H. Lessin
First published in 2011, this text acknowledges the reality and challenges of mature economies and seeks to identify the forces that will drive sustainable growth in the coming decade.

We Can All Do Better by Bill Bradley

Bill Bradley is a wise and engaging voice who continues to be relevant and instructive to leaders today. Bradley served as a U.S. senator from New Jersey from 1979–1997. In 2000, he was a candidate for the Democratic nomination for President of the United States. Before his political career, Bradley was an accomplished basketball player, earning an Olympic gold medal in 1964 and winning two NBA championship rings with the New York Knicks. Bradley has written six books on the topics of culture, economy, and politics in America. This newest text takes a close look at the role of money and politics and the turmoil surrounding financial markets and Washington gridlock.

The 21 Irrefutable Laws of Leadership by John C. Maxwell

With a foreword by Zig Ziglar, this text examines the efforts of some of history's most famous and influential leaders. By reviewing the lives of the famous — including Lee Iacocca, Abraham Lincoln, and Princess Diana — the author shows us how laws of leadership can be gleaned from the actions and experiences of those in the public eye.

On Great Service by Leonard Berry

A collection of stories and analysis focusing on the how-to of great customer service. Berry examined dozens of companies, in a range of sizes and industries, all with reputations for delighting the customer. Berry's onsite observations of firms such as Mary Kay Cosmetics, Tattered Cover Book Store, Longo Toyota & Lexus, Lakeland Regional Medical Center, and Hard Rock Café give the reader real-life examples of superior service in action.

Curated Conversations

While I still think the book is a great format, the digital revolution allows us to converse with thought leaders on an ongoing and dynamic basis. There are many interesting conversations I follow regularly online so I can hear and participate in the latest discussions. Some of my favorite curated conversations take place in blogs led by:

- Seth Godin (http://sethgodin.typepad.com/)
- Barry Ritholtz (http://www.ritholtz.com/blog/)
- David Ignatius (http://www.americanthinker.com)
- Daniel Pink (http://www.danpink.com/)

Index